CAMOUFLAGE CHRISTIANS

Are you hiding from God?

E.M. HOUTZ

ACCENT BOOKS
Denver, Colorado

Unless otherwise noted, all Scripture quotations in this book are from the *Holy Bible, New International Version.* Copyright © 1973, 1978, 1984 International Bible Society. Used by permission of Zondervan Bible Publishers.

ACCENT BOOKS

A division of Accent Publications, Inc.
12100 West Sixth Avenue
P.O. Box 15337
Denver, Colorado 80215

Copyright © 1990 Accent Publications, Inc.
Printed in the United States of America

All rights reserved. No portion of this book may be reproduced in any form without the written permission of the publishers, with the exception of brief excerpts in magazine reviews.

Library of Congress Catalog Card Number 89-82247

ISBN 0-89636-261-2

To the glory of God
and
in memory of
Capt. Robert W. Geeding, USN,
with love to the family

CONTENTS

Introduction:
    I'd Like You to Meet Someone   7

1/ Everybody Knows You Can't Hide from God—Don't They?   13

2/ Hiding Place #1:
    Under the Dresser   21

3/ Hiding Place #2:
    In the Warehouse   36

4/ Hiding Place #3:
    Behind the Photo Album   58

5/ Hiding Place #4:
    Inside the Trophy Case   83

6/ Hiding Place #5:
    Outside the Voting Booth   95

7/ Hiding Place #6:
    Among the Crowd   110

8/ Hiding Place #7:
    Under the Bulldozer   126

9/ Hiding or Seeking:
    What's the Difference?   144

—INTRODUCTION—

I'd Like You to Meet Someone

The Christian life is an adventure, a never-ending expedition of discovery and challenge. It is exciting; it is without limits; it is a life of quiet exultation and dazzling splendor.

God unfolds for each of us individually the infinite dimensions of our walk with Him. The ways He reveals Himself and His lessons to us never cease to amaze me. I believe there is something for us to learn about Him in every experience because each one has the potential to shape who we are.

These lessons don't always come out of easy or joyful circumstances, but they always come if our hearts are open to receiving them.

On January 20, 1989, a US-3 Viking utility aircraft crashed into Subic Bay in the Philippines. Both Naval aviators aboard were killed. One of them was Capt. Robert Geeding, commanding officer of the Fleet Logistics Support Squadron Fifty, based in the Philippines.

Bob Geeding was my cousin; our grandmothers were twin sisters. Born 13 years before me, Bob was the oldest of a close-knit tribe of Indiana cousins with whom I shared the milestones of growing up. Together we swatted mosquitoes and brushed flies off potato salad at summer family reunions on Aunt Coral's lawn. We chased nameless mongrel dogs and wild-eyed cats in and out of uncles' barns. We gathered for Christmas dinners at which turkeys with oyster stuffing, hot vegetables, and sugar cream pies materialized with magical regularity. Sometimes at Easter we assembled, too, just to see what we all looked like dressed up.

Later on, we were together again at the times our grandmothers died. By then, the rest of us had made our way tentatively into adulthood. Bob, of course, had gotten there way ahead of us. While I was still in grade school, he had graduated from college and enlisted in the National Guard and later the Navy. One of the tales in our family's lore tells of the day that, as a young pilot, he sky-wrote the initial "G" over his father's farm.

When I was in high school, Bob served in Vietnam. Later, aboard the *USS Oriskany,* the *Coral Sea*, the *Kitty Hawk*, the *Constellation*. Then, for awhile, in Washington. Two Meritorious Service Medals, 11 Air Medals and the Navy Commendation Medal. Over 5,000 hours of accident-free flight time.

As the forerunner and scout on our collective expedition into the real world, Bob was a very tough act to follow.

He was 51 when he died. The Navy honored him with the flamboyant dignity of full military regalia, befitting his three decades of service. First there was an imposing brass-and-blue funeral in the Philippines, and then another like it in his stateside home, San Diego. A few days later, still another ceremony took place, a memorial service at a little Presbyterian church in the Indiana town near his parent's farm. I was there.

This book was about one-third finished then, well into the subject of how we try to hide ourselves from God and, in doing so, miss out on the excitement of meeting His challenges head-on. At the memorial service, amid the muffled sounds of grief and shock, Bob's friends and colleagues eulogized him. They painted a vivid and affectionate picture of a man I had not seen in over two decades, but who had been my hero since childhood. "That Bob was a hero is undeniable," one of the Navy officers said, "but there was more to him than that. Much more."

They went on to fill in the picture of a man who lived without hiding, without trying to evade what God had called him to do and to be. They portrayed a man who did not hide from danger, from duty, or from the needs of those under his command or in his personal life. They spoke of a man who sought the best in others and always gave the best of what God had enabled him to be. Above all, they told us of a man ferociously and passionately convinced that every day is to be lived, not just endured, and that the living is an adventure.

Bob's light was not a candle, burning unnoticed in its candlestick, but a star—dazzling, glowing, radiant against the background of a dark world. Not hidden, but mounted, literally, in the skies.

Bob's daughter, Pamela Geeding Hartsuyker, wrote a poem about him that began,
> *He lived a life on the edge of silver wings;*
> *Never fearing the consequences....*

What a glorious image: living life "on the edge of silver wings"—a fearless, bold, courageous life. Surely that's the life of faithful adventuring to which God calls us.

Not all of us have the stuff or the desire to choose the life Bob chose. But each of us has the same kind of choice: to live the adventure God places before us, or to hide from Him amid the circumstances of our lives, the people and the relationships, the roles, the tasks, and the busy-ness. We can hide in our own uncertainty about what He would have us do, or we can say,"Here I am, Lord," and wait expectantly on Him. We can hide from Him or we can run headlong, with anticipation and courage, into the exciting business of living for Him.

The light within us can be a candle, feebly burning, easily extinguished by adversity or neglect. Or it can be a star, ignited by the Holy Spirit and fueled by a sense that life is exciting because God challenges us each day to make it so. As in so many things, the choice is ours: to hide or to seek.

Like I said, Bob, you're a tough act to follow. May your life and your memory inspire others to live the adventure.

"Nothing in all creation is hidden from God's sight."
—Hebrews 4:13

— 1 —

Everybody Knows You Can't Hide from God—Don't They?

Everybody knows you can't hide from God. Don't they?

Surely Jack knows. He's a busy executive, working in his office late at night, poring over printouts and making crucial decisions. It's 10 p.m., and he's been at the office since 7 a.m., just like every day this week. Tomorrow he leaves for a three-day business trip. He'll be back for the weekend, have dinner with a visiting client, then dive back into a week of 15-hour workdays. Looks like a hardworking, ambitious fellow, not like someone who's hiding from God.

Let's take another look.

When the church needs someone with financial management experience to head up the budget committee, everyone can see Jack's far too busy. When it's time for his teenage son to start dating and to be taught about morality in relationships, well, Jack has too many things on his mind so his wife will have to handle it. And when some preacher starts to raise tough questions about the meaning of life, Jack won't have to wrestle with the answers. His work is the most important thing in his life, and he has all the answers he needs to succeed in that.

"What do you mean, I'm 'hiding from God'?" Jack will ask you indignantly. "I go to church. I contribute to the offering. Listen! It takes a lot of hard work to get to the top and stay there, and that's what I intend to do."

Or, what about Irene, whose dedicated volunteer efforts are a legend in the community? Surely no one would suggest that *she's* hiding from God. Her fund-raising efforts for the Free Clinic and her management of the hospital's volunteer corps have put her on every organization's most-wanted list. The newspaper has published articles about her, and she's won all kinds of awards for community service. A person who's done so much for the welfare of others surely must be a Christian, not someone who's hiding from God.

"I just don't believe in sitting back and letting other people do all the work, " Irene says. "My religion is doing for others, like the Golden Rule says. I think that's a lot more important than reading the Bible and going to church. Besides, I get uncomfortable when people start a lot of pious talk about 'inviting Christ into your life'; I'd rather be out there *doing* something. I believe religion is a personal thing, and that all you have to do to get to heaven is to lead a good life."

Everyone knows you can't hide from God, yet, Jack is using his work as a hiding place, while Irene is using good deeds—worthwhile though they are.

What about you and me? We may know Christ personally. But do we still try to hide?

We may try to hide in our roles as parents or working people, among our material possessions, behind our accomplishments, or even amid a lot of apparently religious activity. All of these things are within our control. We like to be in charge. But the Bible tells us that the first step in salvation as well as Christian maturity is relinquishing control, saying, "Not as I will, but as you will" (Matthew 26:39).

It's so much easier to hide.

Trying to hide from God isn't new, though. Men and women have been working at it for thousands of years!

Imagine that old character, Jonah, thinking he could hide from God by taking a sea cruise. Did he really believe that if he sailed to another part of the world, God wouldn't be able to find him?

And what about that fellow Peter? He'd been at Jesus' side every day, following Him everywhere He went, yet, in the courtyard of Pilate's house, he tried to pass himself off as a casual observer, denying he was ever "one of them." The people around him may have believed it, but did he really think *God* wouldn't recognize him?

Look at Moses, the mighty leader who brought his people out of slavery. Even he tried to dodge God's plans for him. When God told him to bring the Israelites out of Egypt, Moses' response was, "Why me?" When God instructed him to tell the Egyptians what would happen if they failed to let the Israelites go, his reaction was, "What if they don't believe me?" Finally, after God had spelled out all the things He wanted Moses to do, Moses begged Him, "O Lord, please send someone else to do it." Maybe he thought he could just go back to tending his father-in-law's sheep, and someone else could deliver Israel. But that's not the way it happened.

Everyone knows you can't hide from God—or do they?

Like our world today, the Bible is filled with stories of men and women who tried in dozens of ways to hide from God—not always to hide physically, like Jonah, but to hide spiritually. They tried to hide by ignoring God's laws and pursuing their own human desires. They tried to hide by surrounding themselves with wealth and prestige as substitutes for commitment. They tried to hide by worshiping idols so they could disregard God's commandments.

It's hard to imagine that they really thought they could successfully hide from God. Or is it?

Those biblical characters tried to escape God's claim on their lives.

We, too, may try to find ways to avoid the challenges He gives to us.

While a part of us acknowledges that we cannot hide from God in any real physical or spiritual sense, our willful, sinful human nature still tries.

Why?

We hide because we are afraid to face ourselves in the mirror God holds up. The standard God has set for us by Christ's example and in His word is a lofty one. We fear that, measured against His standards, our lives, our thoughts, and our actions will be found wanting. The idea of not measuring up doesn't appeal to us—or our pride or self-sufficiency. But if you don't try, you can't fail—so we stay away from people, ideas, and information that might force us to compare ourselves to God's standards and become the men and women God wants us to be.

We hide because we are afraid of what God might call us to do. If we obey His command to "seek," and to "ask," we run the risk that we won't like what we find. We've made our own plans, and we don't want God meddling in them, jeopardizing our earthly security or thwarting our ambition. The Christian life is one of joy and victory, but it is also one of obedience and sacrifice. If I ask for God's will to be done in my life, that may mean I won't get what I want.

We hide because of the pressure of others' opinions. We care what others think of us. Their opinions, their esteem, and their resulting actions affect us in powerful ways. They can hurt us and belittle us if they choose to do so. We don't want to willingly make ourselves vulnerable to that. Belonging, being accepted as part of the group, is a fundamental need. What if I express opinions or beliefs others disagree with or even ridicule? What if I don't go along with the crowd? I might find myself alone.

We hide because we lack a sense of our place in God's plan. Somehow we have come to view Christian commitment as just one item on life's smorgasbord of choices, instead of as an absolute claim on our lives. We fail to sense the intensity of God's love for us and the fact that He equips us specially and uniquely to serve Him.

We hide because we overestimate our own achievements. Sometimes, instead of having a too-low estimate of ourselves, we over-value our capabilities. We begin to believe we can hide from God because we don't need Him. Why should we go to the trouble of doing what He wants us to when we can get along so well without Him? Of course, this thinking ignores the fact that any abilities, talents, physical health, material gain, and even the very hours and minutes of our days are only entrusted to us temporarily by God for His honor and glory. They're not ours at all.

We hide because we want to avoid adversity. We are afraid of martyrdom, discomfort, and personal sacrifice. The cost of "picking up the cross" to follow Christ frightens us. It produces conflict and struggle both outside and within us. The battle between our will and God's will can escalate to all-out war that tears us apart; why subject ourselves to that? And why risk having to defend our convictions to those around us—even (shudder) to the point of death?

It's no wonder that sometimes we're tempted to hide, to run away to something or someplace where it seems like life will be easier and less demanding. We may not even recognize that's what we're doing. Those around us may not be able to tell when we're hiding from God. But, *He* knows.

Then, maybe we're not hiding completely. Maybe we're only hiding some aspect of our lives. Maybe we're willing to live by God's guidelines in our personal lives, but in business, well, there's a whole different set of rules. Or maybe we prefer to follow biblical standards in our business, but write our own rules for sexual relationships. Our complex and fast-paced world offers lots of hiding places and lots of temptations to hide.

Sometimes we choose to hide because it's just easier. Sometimes it's more convenient. Sometimes it's a way of protecting a lifestyle or a relationship or something else that we feel, deep down, God would ask us to give up.

God's expectation of us is tough: Be godly people in an ungodly world. Seek spiritual riches while surrounded by material temptations. Measure success by Christ's standards while those around us measure it in dollars or titles or power. Be faithful to our Christ-based commitments when others are more than willing to compromise.

We've all done it, at one time or another. The problem is that when we hide from God, we miss out on the richness and fulness of life He wants us to have. We lose the opportunity to experience the many dimensions of committed Christian living. We forfeit the privileges of being His children. . .privileges that include:

■ *Power*. When we come out of hiding, ready to accept the challenges God has for us, He empowers us to do things we could never begin to do on our own. He enables us to overcome obstacles with courage; to take risks with optimism; to seize opportunities with excitement; to face trouble with faith; to live our day-to-day lives with serenity and confidence. His power becomes perfect in our impotence (II Corinthians 12:8).

This power, though, doesn't conform to the world's definition. The power God gives us enables us to achieve His ends, not our own; it is power that we neither create nor control. It doesn't result from strength but from acknowledging our weakness. It comes to us not when we strive to be masters but when we accept the role of servants. It's power that changes lives and hearts and advances God's work on earth. In short, it is power the world can only dream of having, and it's the only kind of power truly worth having.

■ *Meaning and purpose.* By coming out of hiding, we exchange lives of reacting to what happens around us for lives with a sense of destination, of purpose. We trade delusions about our own importance for positive assurance that we have a special place in this world and a special role to fulfill.

■ *Wholeness.* When we stop hiding behind earthly roles, identities, or expectations, we free ourselves to become the uniquely-crafted creatures God designed us to be. We maximize our talents and integrate the many dimensions of our lives into a whole that is infinitely greater than the sum of its many parts.

■ *Sonship.* God calls us to be His children (Romans 8:14-17). That's His claim on our lives, and that's the identity He offers us. Through Christ we can enjoy not only the privileges of God's loving Fatherhood during our earthly lives, but we also inherit the promise of eternity. Isn't it amazing that some still try to hide from Him?

Adam and Eve, of course, were the first people to try to hide from God. After they ate the fruit God had expressly forbidden, they "heard the sound of the Lord God as he was walking in the garden in the cool of the day, and they hid from the Lord God among the trees of the garden. But the Lord God called to the man, 'Where are you?' " (Genesis 3:8-9).

It's interesting that God called to them, because He already knew where they were. No one is hidden from Him. But, by calling to them, God compelled them to come out of hiding, to reveal themselves and to take a stand before Him.

Like Adam and Eve, we are never truly hidden from God, either. And He calls to us to come out of hiding and to stand before Him, to give an account of our lives as faithful or unfaithful stewards (I Corinthians 4:1-5). Because of Christ, when we respond to God's call to come out of hiding, we enter into an eternal partnership and a lifetime of challenge and discovery.

Wherever and however we try to hide, God will find us. He sees into our hearts; He will challenge us, chasten us, encourage us—and unfailingly love us.

The coming chapters look at the many ways men and women today try to hide from God. Examine your own hiding places, then consider what it would mean to respond to God's call and to come out of those hideouts, to meet the challenges He chooses to set before you.

When we walk in the light, we walk in the constant, loving presence of God, of Christ, and of the Holy Spirit. But when we try to hide, it's lonely.

— 2 —
Hiding Place #1: Under the Dresser

Playing the Game

My grandparents' huge, old house was an ideal place to play hide-and-seek. The rooms were filled with massive pieces of Victorian furniture that could easily hide a child who crept behind or under them. My sister and I soon learned, though, that hiding in any of the bedrooms held a strategic pitfall. In each bedroom, a huge mirror was mounted over the dresser. The unsuspecting hider, thinking her opponent couldn't see her, would venture to peek out of her hiding place, only to see herself reflected in the mirror at the same time her opponent did, and aha! The game was up.

We readily concluded that the safest hiding place in the bedrooms was under the dresser where there was no danger of being seen in the mirror. Of course, once we'd drawn that conclusion, under the dresser was the first place the seeker would look and, therefore, it became worthless as a hiding place.

The Mirror: Ruthless, But Reliable

In my sister's and my game of hide-and-seek, being reflected in the mirror meant sure discovery. It revealed us, took away the protection of our hiding place. We

us, took away the protection of our hiding place. We learned quickly to avoid the mirror.

In our day-to-day lives, a mirror sometimes shows us unpleasant things. It tells us the spaghetti sauce we had for lunch has found its way to our blouse or tie; we stayed up too late last night and have bluish bags under our eyes to show for it; we need a haircut, a shave, or to comb our hair. The old saying that "the mirror doesn't lie" is, unfortunately, one of the more accurate cliches in our language.

The mirror tells us the truth about ourselves. It gives us a chance to measure the reality of how we look against the expectations and standards of how we *want* to look.

The Bible uses the mirror as a symbol of God's expectations and standards for us, too, expressed in His Word and through His Spirit. This "mirror" doesn't lie, either. When we look at our reflection in it, we see that we fall short of the standards God has set for us. And, just as when we look into a glass mirror, we may not like what we see.

As a result, we may try to hide "under the dresser." In order to avoid being reflected unfavorably in the mirror of God's commands and principles, we simply avoid placing ourselves in a position to be seen, either by ourselves or by others. We may go to church, but we listen to the sermon without considering how it applies to us. We avoid in-depth Bible study because learning more about what God wants from us creates demands we don't want to meet.

The Apostle James describes it this way:

Anyone who listens to the word but does not do what it says is like a man who looks at his face in a mirror and, after looking at himself, goes away and immediately forgets what he looks like (1:23-24).

This person forgets he has spaghetti sauce on his tie or

needs to visit the barber. He knows what he needs to change, but he walks away and forgets.

Another way of staying safely under the dresser is simply to make sure we don't expose ourselves to information or open ourselves up to knowledge of what God wants of us.

Non-Christians play the game, too. A man I know, a hard-working, ambitious, successful professional, absolutely refuses to discuss spiritual matters. In spite of many years of friendship, when he is with my family and the conversation turns to spiritual things, he employs a whole arsenal of tactics to avoid considering God's claim on his life.

One of his tactics is the use of pseudo-logic: "I don't see how any intelligent, rational human being can believe all that stuff," he says. Another is sarcasm: "Adam and Eve? A flood? A guy inside a whale? Give me a break." Another technique he uses is asking questions he knows cannot be answered out of earthly wisdom or apart from faith: "If God is so loving, why does He allow such suffering in the world?"

He pokes fun at people who express their faith freely, and abruptly cuts off conversations when they veer into spiritual subjects. He has become highly skilled at steering clear of any information that might challenge the view he has chosen to take of the world.

Christians, on the other hand, sometimes hide "under the dresser" by clinging tightly to our idea of who and what we are. We say things like, "That's just the way I am; I've always been that way," or "Well, there's nothing I can do about it; some things just can't be changed." We may even try to blame our behavior on someone else. We explain that if our spouses, co-workers, bosses, children, parents, or anyone else would change, then we could be better people. These strategies enable us to remain in our current ways of thinking and behaving, so that we won't have to face the possibility that we need to change something about ourselves.

After all, a look in the mirror usually prompts us to take action to correct something. Most of us, seeing problems revealed, wouldn't just walk away and forget what we'd seen; we'd do something about it. We want to look good.

A woman who used to work for me was lamenting her lack of ability to organize her time and her work. "I just seem to let everything get so disorganized," she said. "Then before I know it, everything's out of control. Assignments are late, and I'm not on top of anything. You seem to have a real knack for organization. Have you always been so super-organized?"

Although I was flattered by her remark, it made me laugh inwardly. The truth is that I have had to learn to be well organized, and the lessons came through painful trial, error, and much, much hard work. By nature I'm a chronically and contentedly disorganized person; but when I compared my nature to the standards of what was needed to do my job well, it was clear that I had to learn some new skills of organization.

It wasn't a quick-fix situation, either. Overcoming my natural inclination toward disorder took constant work and discipline—and still does. I wasn't able to overcome it once and for all through some magical technique or dynamic training seminar. It was, and still is, a continual challenge for me.

The changes we need to make in our spiritual lives often follow that same pattern. The war between our old nature and the new nature Christ gives us goes on and on. It doesn't end when we've memorized 100 verses of Scripture or shared our testimony with 25 people. The process of change that brings us closer to God's standards is a constant challenge and a lifelong sequence of victories and defeats, both small and great. To keep the process moving and on-course requires that we constantly check our bearings against the standard of God's Word.

"But the man who looks intently into the perfect law that gives freedom, and continues to do this, not forgetting what he has heard, but doing it—he will be blessed in what he does" (James 1:25).

Measuring Up

When we look at ourselves in God's "mirror," what do we see? If we look at our reflection and compare it to what He wants us to be, how do we measure up?

To answer those questions, we have to know what it is God expects of us. He makes that abundantly clear in His Word. But we must go to that "mirror" in disciplined, prayerful, study of the Bible. Only then can we grow to understand what kind of people God wants us to be.

Let's identify and define some of the qualities we would like to see in our reflection. If we know some of the standards God has set for us, when we look at ourselves in the mirror, we'll have a basis for deciding if we're "well-dressed" spiritually.

The Standard of Love :
"Love the Lord your God with all your heart and with all your soul and with all your mind and with all your strength....Love your neighbor as yourself" (Mark 12:30-31).

The Standard of Stewardship:
"No servant can serve two masters. Either he will hate the one and love the other, or he will be devoted to the one and despise the other. You

cannot serve both God and money" (Luke 16:13).

The Standard of Service :
"Whoever wants to be great among you must be your servant, and whoever wants to be first must be slave of all" (Mark 10: 43-44).

The Standard of Faith:
"Now faith is being sure of what we hope for and certain of what we do not see. . . .By faith we understand that the universe was formed at God's command. . ." (Hebrews 11:1,3).

The Standard of Wisdom :
"The fear of the Lord is the beginning of wisdom, and knowledge of the Holy One is understanding" (Proverbs 9:10).

The Standard of Work:
"Whatever you do, work at it with all your heart, as working for the Lord, not for men " (Colossians 3:23).

The Standard of Forgiveness:
"Bear with each other and forgive whatever grievances you may have against one another. Forgive as the Lord forgave you" (Colossians 3:13).

The Standard of Thoughts:
"Whatever is true, whatever is noble, whatever is right, whatever is pure, whatever is lovely, whatever is admirable—if anything is excellent or praiseworthy—think about such things" (Philippians 4:8).

The Standard of Priorities:
"But seek first his kingdom and his righteousness. . ." (Matthew 6:33).

about you, but what I see when I look at myself in God's mirror isn't the same as what's described above.

Nobody likes failure. Nobody wants to begin something, and then not do it well or successfully. I believe that's part of the reason we try to hide from God's mirror: We don't like being reminded that we're not what we should be; that we've failed the One to whom we owe the most.

There is also the frustration of trying to achieve a standard we know we can't reach. Our reflection reveals us as we are and clearly shows that we need to make changes, but we feel so inadequate to meet God's standards. We're almost afraid to commit to trying; we fear the results of not making it. And when we do try, we repeatedly fall short of being the people we'd like to be—and know God wants us to be.

The Apostle Paul expresses this frustration passionately in Romans 7. He talks about the constant struggle within himself: the battle between the part of him that knows the right things to do and wants to do them, and the part of him that just wants whatever "comes naturally" and to live by the world's rules. He speaks for all of us when he says, "I have the desire to do what is good, but I cannot carry it out. For what I do is not the good I want to do; no, the evil I do not want to do—this I keep on doing" (7:18-19).

Can you think of an incident recently in which you knew the right thing to do, but, for whatever reason, just didn't do it? Instead, maybe you did the thing that was most expedient, or easiest, or most popular with those around you. Afterward, maybe you even asked yourself, "Now why did I do that? I know it wasn't the right thing to do, but I did it anyway. What's the matter with me?" It's an uncomfortable feeling, often accompanied by guilt.

So—to avoid this sense of failure and frustration, we try

So—to avoid this sense of failure and frustration, we try to avoid anything that reminds us of what God expects us to be and do.

God doesn't see us as failures, though. Failure is a human notion, not a divine one. God knows our limitations and fully understands that we cannot attain the perfection of His standards for us: "For all have sinned and fall short of the glory of God" (Romans 3:23). That's why He extends His grace to us—because if we had to rely on our own abilities to measure up, no one would ever make the grade! "Blessed is the man whose sin the Lord will never count against him" (Romans 4:8).

God's grace is a reflection of His love and kindness. It can be a very difficult concept for us to understand, because it doesn't conform to the world's philosophy.

A couple I know, Ron and Karen, made a major financial investment a few years ago. They took some money they had been saving "for a rainy day" and invested it in a venture being put together by a local entrepreneur whom they had met through Karen's job. They were told they could expect a significant return on their investment within two to three years. Two years later, however, they learned that the company involved had been so severely mismanaged that not only would they never see their investment again, but there was a chance they could be called on to make good the enormous debts the company's management had incurred.

"I've learned something from this," Ron said ruefully. "You know that saying, 'There's no such thing as a free lunch?' Well, it's true. I should have known right away that this thing sounded too good to be true."

We have grown cynical. Our experiences in the world have made us suspicious of things that sound too good to be true. Based on Ron's experience, perhaps that suspicion is healthy in many situations. But God doesn't operate by the world's rules. When He offers us grace through Christ to cover our sins, there's no catch, no hidden agenda. His love is unconditional. We have only to accept, to say "yes" to Christ.

"But when the kindness and love of God our Savior appeared, he saved us, not because of righteous things we had done, but because of his mercy" (Titus 3:4).

God saved us "not because of righteous things we had done," but because He loves us. He had compassion upon our fallen race and sent His only Son to pay the penalty our sin deserved. We don't have to live up to God's perfect standards to earn His grace; He gives it to us freely. So when, as His children, we try to live lives pleasing to Him, it's not a futile striving to be "good enough" but an outgrowth of the knowledge that by living according to His commands, we can experience the full, godly lives He wants for us.

As we seek to live that life everyday, we have God's Word to guide us, Christ's example to encourage us, and the Holy Spirit to empower us. We really can't lose!

Picture-Perfect

In my short-but-exhausting experience in an aerobics class, I learned the value of using a mirror to check my own progress. The room where the class was held had mirrors covering one wall. The students would watch the teacher perform a certain routine and then try it ourselves. Only by looking in the mirror could I tell whether what I was doing had any resemblance to what the teacher had demonstrated. (It generally didn't.)

The mirrors wouldn't have been any help, though,

without the teacher's demonstration. Without having seen what the routine was supposed to look like, we'd have no way of knowing whether we were doing it properly.

Christ's life was a demonstration of the life God wants us to live. In Him we can see what God's standards look like in action. By studying His example and trying to live as He did, we move closer to being the people God wants us to be. And when we fail to make Christ-like choices or to speak, think and act in Christ-like ways—which we do, time and time again—then by God's grace we can try again, knowing He still loves us.

Hopefully, each time we look in the mirror, we'll see a little more of Christ reflected in us, and, at the same time, we'll reflect more of Christ to those around us.

Just a Reminder

In my aerobics class, the teacher didn't simply demonstrate each routine one time and then stop, leaving us to flounder on our own until we perfected it for ourselves. Seeing it performed just one time wasn't enough to enable the rest of us to master it. She would lead us through each routine several times, repeating various parts of it when needed and prodding us along when we forgot what came next. As we practiced, she would walk among the students, offering suggestions and encouragement, correcting mistakes, and reminding us of the right form and technique.

God isn't a one-time Teacher, either. When Christ left this earth, men and women no longer had His physical presence, His observable example, to guide them in their day-to-day lives. So God sent us another Teacher, a Counselor to encourage us, to point out mistakes, and to remind us of the Father's expectations.

"And I will ask the Father, and he will give you

> *another Counselor—the Spirit of truth. . . . You know him, for he lives with you and will be in you. I will not leave you as orphans. . . . But the Counselor, the Holy Spirit, whom the Father will send in my name, will teach you all things and remind you of everything I have said to you"* (John 14:16-18a,26).

Jesus did not leave us "as orphans." He did not abandon us to struggle alone in our weakness and our limited understanding, trying futilely to remember and obey the things He told us. Instead, He sent the Spirit of truth who would not only be *with* us, but would *live in* us, to teach and guide us.

The world around us can be very deceptive. So much that is valued by the world is worthless by God's standards. So much that is believed to be true is false in God's eyes. So much that is said to be right is wrong by God's ethics.

Yet, amid all the potentially deceptive forces, here we are, armed with the Spirit of truth within us. What a source of strength and courage when we feel like we're swimming upstream against the tide of "popular" opinion.

For instance, as a parent, I find it hard to know where to draw the line regarding what magazines, movies, and television shows I let my son see. I simply believe that an 11-year-old child does not need to be exposed to the hateful, violent, profane, and tasteless material that fills much of the media today. There is enough ugliness around us without willingly exposing ourselves to fictional portrayals of it (and paying to do so!).

However, when I veto his requests to see certain shows until I have had a chance to preview them first, his response is often, "All my friends have seen it." Even parents whose judgment and opinion I respect are often more lenient in this area than I am. I begin to wonder if I'm wrong. Maybe I'm being too strict. Maybe he needs to be exposed to what's out there in the world to avoid growing up naive and ignorant. I feel like I'm standing alone, fighting the majority opinion and losing.

This is only one small issue among the countless dilemmas of being a parent! I find it immeasurably reassuring to know that somewhere in me, even though it may be buried beneath all my human frailties and limitations, the Spirit of truth resides. Even when popular opinion says, "Go ahead; let him see what he wants." Another small voice says, "Remember this: 'whatever is true, whatever is noble, whatever is right, whatever is pure, whatever is lovely, whatever is admirable'—these are the things with which we should fill our minds" (from Philippians 4:8).

The next time you face a difficult decision, and feel like the accepted or popular answer might just be easier than the right one, listen for the Spirit of truth speaking to you. The world can't and won't hear it, but you can. Listen patiently. Listen quietly. Listen openly. Christ promised the Spirit would teach us all things and remind us of everything He said to us—and that the Spirit would empower us to do what God wants.

We don't have to rely on our own limited wisdom or strength to live for God in an ungodly world. In fact, we can't; it won't work. But the Holy Spirit, like a mirror, enables us to "see" ourselves and prompts us to make the changes that will bring us closer to that standard. Then, He empowers us to live more wholly for Him.

"And this is how we know that he lives in us: We know it by the Spirit he gave us" (I John 3: 24).

Are You Seeing Red?
What happens when we don't listen to the Spirit's voice?

What happens when, in spite of our good intentions, we do the wrong thing? What happens when, because we are imperfect, we sin?

What happens when the reflection in the mirror is so far from what we know God wants that we don't even want to look?

God, in His wisdom, has covered this eventuality, too. He knows it will happen to us. We make bad choices. We take the easy route instead of the conscientious one. We say "okay" when deep down we know we shouldn't. How can we face God again?

We can face God because Christ is our advocate. When we don't follow Christ's example, when we disregard the counsel of the Holy Spirit and succumb to the old nature in each of us—even then we have hope. We have the assurance of our salvation and a chance to keep on striving to become the people God wants us to be.

"My dear children, I write this to you so that you will not sin. But if anybody does sin, we have one who speaks to the Father in our defense—Jesus Christ, the Righteous One. He is the atoning sacrifice for our sins, and not only for ours but also for the sins of the whole world" (I John 2:1-2).

Wow! What a promise.

You Can Come Out Now

Statistics are important to the business I am in. Several years ago I contacted a research firm about designing a survey that would help our company evaluate the success of a certain project. My hope, of course, was that the survey results would show that the program had successfully met its goals.

After I explained the program at length to the researcher and described the type of survey I envisioned, he asked, "What do you expect the results to show?"

"Well," I said, "I suppose I expect them to show that the program was successful."

"Based on what you've told me," he replied, "I think it's unlikely that the data from this type of survey would turn out the way you want. That doesn't mean the program hasn't been successful. It's just that measuring the kind of results you're looking for with this type of survey is difficult, and the data may end up looking much less positive than you're expecting."

I thought about what he had said, then thanked him for his candor and decided to postpone the survey for a year, to give the program time to become better established. It didn't seem to make good sense to carry out a survey before the results were tested by time. The bottom line was that the results might, in some way, reflect poorly on me since I had headed up the project.

In other words, as much as I hate to admit it, I "hid under the dresser" in regard to that survey. I didn't want to risk having the survey data reflect something that didn't measure up to expectations.

Most of us do the same thing in our spiritual lives from time to time. In spite of all the ways God shows His love and compassion in dealing with our imperfections and our failures, we spend a certain amount of time under the dresser, trying to avoid facing our reflection in the mirror.

Think about it. What circumstances or events make *you* want to hide under the dresser?

Like many people, I'm tempted to hide when I see a graphic portrayal of the poverty, disease, and squalor of the Third World. It's much easier to close the newspaper or turn off the TV than to figure out what I can do that would make a difference. I also know that if I check my reflection against God' standard, I might see a person who hasn't fully obeyed the command to care for those in need (James 2).

Some people want to hide when their minister or the church stewardship committee starts to talk about sacrificial giving. They don't want to be asked to give up some other use of their financial resources. Some people want to hide when the subject of sexual morality comes up. They fervently agree that killing someone or worshiping idols is wrong, but when it comes to God's clear-cut rules for sexual relationships, they'd rather not listen.

Other people want to hide from challenges to their business practices. They'd never steal their neighbor's stereo, but they don't want to think about whether padding an expense account or a client's bill is really right in God's eyes.

Are you hiding from God's challenge to be Christ-like? If we come out from under the dresser and look in the mirror, we'll see some imperfect people, spaghetti stains and all. But we'll also have the chance to see people of promise, people in whom the Spirit of truth resides, people for whom Christ died. We'll see people God has created with a unique potential to do great things for Him.

Isn't that worth taking a look?

— 3 —
Hiding Place #2:
In the Warehouse

A few months ago my son started saving his money for a video game he wanted to buy. He was constantly asking my husband and me to assign extra chores that he could do to earn additional money. One Sunday morning, as we were preparing to go to church, I said to him," Be sure to take a tithe from the money you've earned doing chores so you can add it to your offering at church."

He was horrified.

"I can't do that!" he said in a panic-stricken voice.

"Why?" I asked him.

"Because then I won't have enough to buy what I want."

Does the expression "from the mouth of babes" come to mind? My son expressed an attitude that most of us, as adults, share. The difference is that he admitted it—and we usually don't.

Learning to manage our material possessions in a way pleasing to God is one of the most difficult aspects of Christian discipleship. It's an uphill climb that makes us fight every step of the way to overcome the pressures of the world around us.

God calls us to careful stewardship and constant self-discipline in relation to worldly gain. The Bible warns us repeatedly of the perils of materialism and the imperma-

repeatedly of the perils of materialism and the impermanence of earthly attainments (I Timothy 6:3-7). "Some people, eager for money, have wandered from the faith and pierced themselves with many griefs" (6:10b). But it's so much easier to hide in our personal warehouses. There, we can surround ourselves with material possessions, the tangible symbols of our achievements, the visible things that feed our self-esteem and egos.

But I Like It In Here!

This particular hiding place has three primary attractions.

First, we can devote so much time and effort to accumulating, maintaining, and managing our possessions that we don't have time to worry about stewardship or spiritual discipline. We can tell ourselves we'll worry about that later, after we've reached a certain income level or a certain stage in our careers. Maybe after the kids are grown or the house or the car is paid off. Maybe then we'll give more to the church or devote less time to making money.

Maybe.

Second, the "warehouse" is a very comfortable hiding place. Life is good there. We have lots of things to give us pleasure and to distract us from the demands of discipleship. The world is always ready to sell us something new for our consumption and enjoyment. More expensive cars. More modern appliances. More elaborate vacations. Clothes that make us look sexier or more successful or more sophisticated. Furniture, stereo equipment, coffeemakers, food products, giant-screen TVs, anything that will impress our neighbors more.

Third, when we hide in the warehouse, the world applauds us, even envies us. Material possessions and monetary wealth are the world's measure of a person's value and accomplishments. They're visible signs to the world that we're "OK." Our society doesn't challenge us to come out of our warehouses; it says, "More is always better."

Water, Water Everywhere

Someone named Elena taught me an important lesson about the comforts of the warehouse.

In October of 1984, my family and I moved into a new house. It wasn't a house you'd ever see in a home decorating magazine (especially after we filled it with our early-attic period furniture) but it was still my "dream house," a symbol for me of permanence and belonging. Unfortunately, the house is located in what the federal government describes as a "flood-prone area."

In September of 1985, when we had lived in our house less than a year, Hurricane Elena swept across Florida's west coast. As she went by, she filled my dream house with filthy, foul-smelling sea water washed up out of Tampa Bay via the city's sewer system. The salty water killed most of the foliage in the yard. It corroded the electrical systems of my appliances. It destroyed the wood paneling and left stains on the plaster walls.

The neighborhood had been evacuated at the time of the flood, and virtually all the residents returned after the evacuation to find water still standing in their houses. I picked up my typewriter—a Christmas gift from my husband—and watched muddy water drain out of it. Treasured books, my son's toys, stuffed animals, shoes—anything that had been on or near the floor was soaked. You can imagine my feelings when I found my waterlogged Bible, the one I'd had for over a decade, with all the margin notes I've taken during Bible studies and sermons. (Fortunately, I was able to dry it out and salvage it.)

My husband and I went through the house with trash bags, filling them with our ruined possessions. The trash collection men found themselves faced with mountains of discarded items outside every house in the neighborhood. Appliances, carpeting, furniture, books, stereo equipment—it looked like each house was having a massive yard sale. I cried a lot during that time, overcome by an aching sense of loss and exhausted by the massive cleanup.

Looking back, I know the damage to my house could have been much worse. The roof could have fallen in or the foundation washed away, as it did at some of the houses on our nearby beaches. A family member could have been hurt or killed. Still, what happened to my house was enough to teach me an unforgettable lesson about trying to hide in the warehouse of material possessions: our hiding place can be gone in an instant. A fire, a flood, a serious financial loss, a robbery—we can lose our possessions so very, very easily.

It took about six months for life to get back to normal after the flood. The insurance adjustors came through. We planted some new foliage and replaced paneling and carpeting. And we cleaned. (And cleaned. And cleaned.)

I still love my house, and I take joy in many of the things I own. My wedding album. The dining room set from my grandmother's house. A souvenir T-shirt from a theme park. My collection of seashells. But Elena taught me that these things can disappear, and life will go on without them. Sometimes I find myself tempted to look for my sense of security among the familiar surroundings of my home. But then I pick up my Bible, with its rippled, water-stained pages and un-glued binding, and I remember that the warehouse is a very unsatisfactory hiding place.

For those of us who face the temptation to hide in our

warehouses, the Bible issues a threefold challenge:

1. The challenge to consecrate all that we have to God.

Harriet is a lively, gray-haired woman who, at the age of 80, hasn't been to church in half a century, except to attend her friends' funerals and her children's and grandchildren's weddings. I asked her once why she never went to church.

"Because they're always asking for money," she replied indignantly.

Harriet isn't the only person I've heard say that. I imagine you've heard it lots of times, too. In fact, if you and I had a dollar for every time we've heard someone say that, we'd be able to support a whole flock of missionaries for years!

Hearing people object to going to church on the grounds that "they're always asking for money" makes me wonder about their logic. Do they assume that (a) God's work on earth doesn't require money, or that (b) the church doesn't have the right to ask us for our money, or that (c) the church should find some way to obtain the money it needs without asking for it, or that (d) if God wanted our money, He'd just take it?

Maybe they just tell themselves, "I've worked for what I have and, by golly, I'm going to keep it."

The question is: How can we expect to "keep" what is not ours to begin with? Even the Old Testament writers saw the error of this line of reasoning. When we devote what we have to God's use—whether our money, our time, our talents, or our possessions—we are only returning a part of what He has entrusted to us.

The Apostle James said, "Don't be deceived, my dear brothers. Every good and perfect gift is from above, coming down from the the Father..." (1:16-17).

We come out of hiding in our warehouses when we

accept the challenge of obedience, the challenge of setting a priority on following God's commandments and living His promises. This commitment liberates us from being entangled by money and material considerations. It gives us a new perspective that realigns all our thinking. We begin to live our spiritual adventure in newfound freedom and excitement.

2. The challenge to share with others.

The Bible clearly commands us to share our money and goods with others. In the Old Testament, God challenged the Israelites to provide for the needs of "the Levites (who have no allotment or inheritance of their own) and the aliens, the fatherless and the widows who live in your towns..." (Deuteronomy 14: 29). The Apostle Paul's letters often refer to the generosity of the believers in various churches who supported him and his fellow missionaries.

> "We want you to know," he wrote to the believers at Corinth, "about the grace that God has given the Macedonian churches. Out of the most extreme trial, their overflowing joy and their extreme poverty welled up in rich generosity. For I testify that they gave as much as they were able, and even beyond their ability" (II Corinthians 8:1-3).

In describing the giving spirit of the Macedonian believers, Paul said, "...they gave themselves first to the Lord and then to us in keeping with God's will" (II Corinthians 8: 5).

They gave themselves first to the Lord.

When we emerge from the warehouse and take that first all-important step—consecrating ourselves to God—then the second step—consecrating all we have to Him—follows. His challenge to the Corinthians rings down through the centuries to us today: "See that you also excel in this grace of giving" (8:7).

A few weeks ago, I was driving down one of the highways that runs through our city and saw a man walking backward along the side of the road, holding up a cardboard sign for passing motorists to see. The man was barefoot; he had long, unkempt-looking hair and was dressed in a grimy undershirt and torn jeans. The awkwardly hand-lettered sign he was holding said,"WILL WORK FOR FOOD."

We don't have to look to the Third World to find people in need, although the need there is unquestionably great. In our own hometowns, our churches, our neighborhoods, there are people without food or warm clothes; sick children lie in unheated homes or sleep in the street because they have no homes at all. When we come out of hiding, we accept God's challenge to meet the needs of others, to give of what we have in a spirit of joy, generosity, and willing sacrifice (II Corinthians 8:10-12). When we come out of hiding, we give because the need is there and we have the means to meet it, not because someone will be impressed by our generosity or awed by our wealth.

Christian giving is not an option; it's an integral part of the package. When we make the decision to allow Christ's sovereignty in our lives, we consecrate all that we are and have to His use. Those things are only under our trusteeship for His use anyway. But now He can trust us to determine, under His guidance, where and how they can best be used to meet the needs of His work and His world. That's stewardship.

3. The challenge to look beyond the material.

Let's go back to the game of hide-and-seek. Unless you had an exceptionally strategic hiding place, one of the problems was that when you were hiding, you couldn't see out. If you hid in a closet or cupboard, you had to keep the door shut. You couldn't look out and see what was going on around you.

Hiding in the warehouse is like that, too. It severely restricts our range of vision. We can see only the things around us, and they block our spiritual vision. When our sight becomes focused on how to get more, earn more, keep more, use more, display more, save more, we lose sight of the less visible but more important realities and values of life.

I like the words the psalmist used to ask God to give him clearer eyesight: "Turn my heart toward your statutes and not toward selfish gain. Turn my eyes away from worthless things; preserve my life according to your word" (Psalm 119:36-37).

This "spiritual blindness" that excessive attention to material things can cause is described in another way in the parable of the sower (Mark 4: 18-19). "Still others, like seed sown among thorns, hear the word; but the worries of this life, the deceitfulness of wealth and the desires for other things come in and choke the word, making it unfruitful."

This parable makes me think of a businessman I used to know. He was brought up in Mississippi, in the heart of the "Bible belt," in a Christian home. He was taught the way to salvation and the principles of the Scriptures. He went to college and entered the business world. He was successful at everything he did. He was intelligent and conscientious in the various jobs he had, moving quickly up the corporate ladder. No amount of hard work was too much for him. Above all, he was gifted with an eye for business opportunities. He put together a small company and bought into other small companies; soon, he was a man of considerable business assets, moving in lofty financial circles.

Somewhere along the line, the things he had been taught as a child were "choked" by the the pressing concerns of business and the striving for success. Even as he accumulated more and more wealth, he had to run faster and faster to keep ahead of his competitors. His church activities fell off. He no longer cared about spiritual growth. He cheated on his wife. His personal devotional life became non-existent. He ridiculed other people who openly expressed their spiritual convictions. The weeds had overgrown the seed.

In spite of all he had attained, he was far from being a happy man. As I grew to know him better, I sensed a restless, discontented spirit and an inner emptiness that no million-dollar sale could fill. I believe that, deep down, he sensed his own emptiness, too. He had been taught the way of salvation, but it was only head knowledge. Someday, he may shake himself free from the weeds, the seeds of his childhood will take root, and God will reap the harvest of his soul. Someday, I hope his life will become like the seed sown on good soil.

What's mine is mine—and I want yours, too.

The ability to see beyond money and material possessions helps protect us from what the Bible calls the love of the world—of which Satan is the master. "Do not love the world or anything in the world. . . .For everything in the world—the cravings of sinful man, the lust of the eyes and the boasting of what he has and does—comes not from the Father but from the world" (I John 2:15-16).

Hiding in the warehouse places us in danger of falling victim to two particular evils: selfishness and greed. The dictionary reflects a difference between selfishness and greed, although both result from self-centeredness rather than Christ-centeredness. Selfishness is defined as a disproportionate concern for one's own interests as opposed to the interests of others; it's a serious case of me-first-ism. Greed, on the other hand, is the desire to have more than your share of whatever is to be had. It's a combination of me-first-ism and more-for-me-ism.

Some years ago, a friend of mine, Kate, was comparing her marriage to that of another couple she knew.

"For example, say Ted and I are finishing dinner, and there are two pieces of cake for dessert, and one's big and one's small. Well, Ted and I would both grab for the larger one for ourselves."

"But not Mike and Alice. They'd both try to take the smaller one, so the other person could have the big one. That's just how they are. It's like they're always wanting more for the other person than for themselves."

Our material possessions and our money are the "cake" in our lives. The way we deal with these things reveals our most basic nature.

Greed is a destructive quality that, in turn, often leads to other immoral behavior. Greed drives us to seek possession of what is not rightfully ours. It leads us to feel we have a "right" to more than we have and more than others have. It distorts our thinking and undermines our positive values. Human greed fosters violence and crime, breaks up marriages and friendships, and causes businessmen and women to break the law. Even Christians who are not on guard against it can find themselves becoming someone they don't want to be.

"Watch out!" Jesus warns us. "Be on your guard against all kinds of greed" (Luke 12:15). Why was Jesus' warning so emphatic? Because He knew greed can lead to idolatry. In fact, the Apostle Paul says they're the same thing: "Put to death, therefore, whatever belongs to your earthly nature: sexual immorality, impurity, lust, evil desires and greed, which is idolatry" (Colossians 3:5).

Hiding in the warehouse obscures our sight of God and His commandments. As we lose touch with that vision, our hearts begin to turn to other gods: money, prestige, a big house, an expensive car...the trappings of worldly success that make other people envy us or stroke our egos with their applause. If this happens, it's time to hit the brakes—hard! "For of this you can be sure," Paul wrote to the Ephesians, "no immoral, impure or greedy person—such a man is an idolater—has any inheritance in the kingdom of Christ and of God" (Ephesians 5:5). Satan's a master deceiver. If we say we're Christians but live like this, the Bible flashes red warning lights.

The world's way is to worship possessions, prestige, status symbols. The Bible says we are to be "imitators of God." It warns us not to conform to the world around us (Romans 12:1-2), just as God warned the Israelites not to follow the practices of the heathen nations surrounding them: "You must not do as they do in Egypt, where you used to live, and you must not do as they do in the land of Canaan, where I am bringing you. Do not follow their practices. You must obey my laws and be careful to follow my decrees. I am the Lord your God" (Leviticus 18:3-4).

Greed is a dangerous, frightening, powerful evil. But the Holy Spirit empowers us to withstand the world's pressure—if we open ourselves to His power.

Selfishness and greed have two other ugly companions, too—competitiveness and strife. This isn't the healthy spirit of competition that prompts us to enter friendly contests in sports, or to compete against another department at work to do a better job. It's an obsessive, win-at-all-costs competitiveness.

The Old Testament tells us a powerful story about competitiveness within a family.

Joseph always got more of everything than his brothers (Genesis 37). His father loved him the most and blatantly showered him with favor and with gifts. The beautiful, multi-colored coat was absolutely the last straw; his brothers just couldn't take any more of Joseph. Their anger, stemming from jealousy and competitiveness over their father's favor, led them to try to destroy their own brother. How easily our destructive emotions can spur us to do things we think we would never dream of doing!

Selfishness and greed invariably lead us into strife, too. Strife is an old-fashioned sounding word we don't hear much today, but we see and feel its presence constantly in our lives and in our world. Strife is conflict between people or groups or nations or between people and circumstances. It's being at war with another person or with an ideology or situation. I picture strife like two pieces of sandpaper being rubbed together; there's friction, roughness, grating. The interaction is never smooth, never harmonious.

Strife appears in the Bible in the company of ugly companions, too. Romans 1:29 lists it along with wickedness, evil, greed, depravity, envy, deceit, and malice. The sinful nature breeds strife because it leads people to pursue only their own desires, without regard for the needs and wants of others. When two co-workers both want a promotion and will do anything to get it, there's strife. When a husband and wife care less about one another's happiness than about their own, there's strife. When people believe they constantly have to get ahead, make more money, gain more power, and out-achieve those around them at any cost, there's strife.

"What causes fights and quarrels among you? Don't they come from your desires that battle within you? You want something but don't get it. You kill and covet, but you cannot have what you

want. You quarrel and fight. You do not have, because you do not ask God. When you ask, you do not receive, because you ask with wrong motives, that you may spend what you get on your pleasures" (James 4:1-3).

Is God in the Banking Business?

The person who hides in the warehouse may well be trying to avoid two basic questions: What would God have me do with the finances and earthly possessions He has allowed me to gain? How do these things fit into His plan for me?

When we make the decision to come out of hiding and emerge from the warehouse, we run headlong into those questions, waiting outside the warehouse door to confront us.

Take tithing, for example. For some, tithing is a scriptural mandate, a non-negotiable facet of Christian life. For others, tithing means giving back to God a tenth of what's left after the bills are paid and the leisure-time activities have been covered. For others, tithing isn't even a part of their spiritual vocabulary.

Sunday offerings and church pledges are the same way, ranging from pocket change that happens to be on the dresser on Sunday morning to a major item in the household budget.

In the contemporary Christian community, attitudes about material wealth run the gamut. At one end is the so-called "prosperity theology," a uniquely American philosophy proposing that God desires all of us to be rich and successful in material terms. At the other extreme is the the renunciation of all worldly possessions, practiced by long-standing religious orders who believe that possession of earthly goods is destructive to spiritual welfare. In between lies a range of spiritual positions nearly as varied as the individual Christians who embrace them.

I don't believe either of these extremes reflect a biblical approach to our stewardship of money or possessions.

Let's examine the Scriptures for some insights, starting with the Old Testament.

The Old Testament writers saw a direct correlation between spiritual obedience and success. God's promise to the people of Israel was, "I will take you as my own people, and I will be your God" (Exodus 6:7). He promised to make Israel a great nation, to free His people from bondage in Egypt, and to give them possession of Canaan. In return, He expected them to obey His commandments—which, the Old Testament tells us, they did with typically human inconsistency.

Deuteronomy 8:17-18 warned God's people: "You may say to yourself, 'My power and the strength of my hands have produced this wealth for me.' But remember the Lord your God, for it is he who gives you the ability to produce wealth." It was not because of their righteousness that God would bless them. No, He told the Israelites clearly that it was because of the wickedness of the nations in Canaan that they would be driven out. The "success" of the Israelites was God's grace to them and His punishment of the wicked people in the land. "Understand then, that it is not because of your righteousness that the Lord your God is giving you this good land to possess, for you are a stiff necked people" (Deuteronomy 9:4-6).

If His people obeyed Him, God would meet their needs.

However, the opposite of this relationship was also true. "If you do not carefully follow all the words of this law, which are written in this book, and do not revere this glorious and awesome name—the Lord your God—the Lord will send fearful plagues on you and your descendants....Just as it pleased the Lord to make you prosper and increase in number, so it will please him to ruin and destroy you" (Deuteronomy 28:58-63).

At the same time, the Old Testament writers acknowledged that the wicked recognized no restrictions on their route to wealth. The psalmist observed that evil men frequently prospered in spite of their wickedness. "In his arrogance the wicked man hunts down the weak, who are caught in the schemes he devises....His ways are always prosperous; he is haughty and your laws are far from him..." (Psalm 10:2,5).

The people of the Old Testament recognized God as sovereign; they knew that He governs all that occurs in the lives of mankind. "...The Lord sends poverty and wealth; he humbles and he exalts" (I Samuel 2:7). "Our God is in heaven; he does whatever pleases him" (Psalm 115:3).

Any material wealth and earthly well-being we experience is simply a gift from God that He gives to us at His pleasure. It is not a symbol of our righteousness or spiritual health. We may work for it, but we don't really earn it. Many godly people work hard and follow His principles for living without accumulating great wealth. Either way, our very ability to do so is a gift from Him, not an achievement of our own. God's definition of success begins with our obedience (Proverbs 21:3) and prosperity is that of the soul who grows rich in the knowledge of God's Word (Joshua 1:7-8; Colossians 1:9-12).

An outgrowth of this sovereignty is the commandment to honor God with our material resources, however big or small they may be. Warehousing our money and possessions for our own use is in direct disobedience to God's desire and command. "Honor the Lord with your wealth, with the firstfruits of all your crops; then your barns will be filled to overflowing, and your vats will brim over with new wine" (Proverbs 3:9-10).

At first glance it might seem that the Old Testament supports "prosperity theology." If we obey God's commandments, we will become materially rich. But there is far more to God's plan for us than that.

Let's look a little more closely at the use of this word "prosper" and related words from the same root: "prosperous," "prosperity," *et cetera*, as well as the Bible's promises of prosperity. Interestingly, in the New International Version (NIV), these words appear 81 times in the Old Testament—and only once in the New! Surely that fact alone tells us that Christ changed man's understanding of the role of "prosperity" in our lives. This idea is further supported by the fact that "wealth" (and related words like "wealthy") appear 111 times in the Old Testament and just 18 times in the New.

In many of the references in the Old Testament, the context of the prosperity words suggests that they do refer specifically to material wealth. An example is Proverbs 11:25: "A generous man will prosper." The *New King James Version* (NKJV) reads, "A generous man will be made rich."

However, in many other cases, the words suggest broader meanings, more closely equivalent to "well-being" than "wealth." For example, in Deuteronomy 5:33, the NIV says, "so that you may live and prosper," but the *New American Standard Bible* (NASB) and the *New King James Version* both say, "that it may be well with you." Similarly, Jeremiah 29:11 in the NIV reads, " 'For I know the plans I have for you,' declares the Lord, 'plans to prosper you and not to harm you, plans to give you hope and a future.' " In the *New American Standard Bible*, the middle portion of the verse reads, "plans for welfare and not for calamity."

In many instances, the word "prosperity" suggests not wealth but well-being.

The first time the word "prosper" occurs in the NIV in the New Testament is in Acts, where Paul is preaching at Pisidian Antioch. He began by saying, " The God of the people of Israel chose our fathers; he made the people prosper during their stay in Egypt" (Acts 13:17). When I first read this verse, it confused me. I thought of the Hebrews in their bitter slavery in Egypt, and I wondered how Paul could possibly describe their condition as prosperous! Then I looked in other translations to see what word was used. The NASB says God "made the people great during their stay in the land of Egypt." God "exalted the people when they dwelt as strangers in the land of Egypt" (NKJ). In this New Testament use, we see another meaning of "prosper"—"to make great"—not necessarily to make great wealth.

When Jesus came into the world, bringing with Him the new covenant between God and man, He also brought a new understanding of the meaning of "prosperity." Jesus made it clear that His purpose was not to undermine or abolish the Old Testament law of the old covenant, but to fulfill it (Matthew 5:17). He came to conquer our sins and to give us spiritual prosperity that we might be acceptable in God's sight. He presented us with a new viewpoint for our spiritual insight.

1. Jesus warns us of the pitfalls of earthly wealth.

While the Old Testament portrays wealth as a positive goal, Jesus constantly warned us of the dangers of too zealous a pursuit. The sad story of the rich young man pictures the choice each of us must make about what will be most important in our lives (Mark 10:17-22). The rich young man had faithfully followed all the religious laws since his childhood. Yet Jesus challenged him to do the one thing that he simply couldn't do: part with his wealth. This parable illustrates the reality that wealth can be an obstacle to obedience rather than a result of it.

In Jesus' challenge to the rich young man to give away all his possessions, the important element wasn't that Jesus was asking this young man to do without material possessions and wealth. The important part is that Jesus knew—because He always knows our hearts—that the young man couldn't give up the things of this world. What God wants isn't for us to give up all our material goods; it's for us to be *willing* to give them up. But notice Christ's clincher to His offer: "Then, come, follow me." That's really what Christ wants—our obedience, *to follow Him.*

Think for a moment about this question:

What use did God have for, say, two or three dozen sheep and a few dozen oxen?

Obviously God had some use for all those sheep, because in Deuteronomy 15:19 He asked for them: "Set apart for the Lord your God every firstborn male of your herds and flocks."

Rev. Marshall McClellan, one of the pastors at my church, raised this question in a recent sermon. He read Deuteronomy 15:19 and then asked, "Now what did God want with all those dirty, smelly sheep and oxen?"

He went on to point out that what God desired from the Israelites was not sheep, or grain, or any of the other firstfruits that the Bible tells us He required of them. He had no use for those things, just as He had no use for the rich young man's possessions or the money you and I place at His altar every Sunday.

These physical things are only symbols.

They are the tangible evidence of our willingness to consecrate or to sacrifice to Him those things that are important to us.

If we cannot separate ourselves from our possessions in this way, and we continue to be bound by them, Jesus says we run another risk: that of being spiritually "choked" by the temptations of wealth and the false values into which it can lead us (Mark 4:7,18-19).

Remember the biblical couple Ananias and Sapphira? What a dramatic lesson this ill-fated pair teaches us!

The community of Jesus' followers at Jerusalem, led by Peter, John, and Barnabas, had agreed to "share everything they had" (Acts 4:32). Members who owned property sold it off from time to time and brought the proceeds to the apostles for distribution as needed. Ananias and Sapphira, however, when they sold a piece of their property, brought only *part* of the money to the community of believers, and kept the rest for themselves. Peter challenged their deception. "How is it that Satan has so filled your heart that you have lied to the Holy Spirit?...You have not lied to men but to God" (Acts 5:3-4). Ananias died on the spot, and a few hours later, when Peter confronted Sapphira in the same way, she, too, fell dead.

The amount of money that was the difference between what Ananias received for his property and what he gave to the church wasn't the issue at all. Like the rich young ruler, Ananias and Sapphira couldn't separate themselves from their wealth; they just couldn't turn over the entire amount to God's work, *but they wanted people to think they had.* The lesson they have for us is one about the temptation to "keep back" a part of what we have, to try to hide it from God's sight and from His use, while we present a hypocritical appearance of godliness.

This is one of the temptations that wealth creates. It tempts us to try to lie to God. We say, "Thy will be done," and then we add silently, "unless it involves giving up something I want." We tell ourselves we are committed to

Him, but at the same time, we reserve certain things as "off limits." We set aside a secret hoard like a Swiss bank account of material goods that we aren't willing to consecrate to Him. We boast about our charity and our support of the church—and we can fool others—but God knows if we are withholding something from Him. He cannot be deceived (Galatians 6:7).

The fate of Ananias and Sapphira illustrates how serious God is about this particular aspect of our spiritual lives. It's a dramatic reminder of just how great is the danger of deceiving ourselves in the comfort of our warehouses.

2. Jesus encourages us to seek the eternal rather than the temporary.

Jesus' teachings redirect our focus from physical well-being in this earthly life to spiritual well-being, both now and in eternity. Obedience, instead of being a means to an end, is an outgrowth of commitment when our sights are set on eternity rather than tomorrow. The parable of the rich farmer who built bigger and bigger barns to store his grain reminds us that no matter how big and full our warehouses grow, we cannot take anything with us into eternity.

"You fool!" God said to the man. "This very night your life will be demanded from you. Then who will get what you have prepared for yourself?" (Luke 12:20).

Jesus calls us to "store up...treasures in heaven" (Matthew 6:20) rather than to invest our energies in accumulating earthly goods that can be easily and suddenly destroyed.

Instead of trusting in riches to bring us joy, safety, or salvation, God commands us to put our hope in Him. "Command those who are rich in this present world not... to put their hope in wealth, which is so uncertain, but to put their hope in God, who richly provides us with everything for our enjoyment" (I Timothy 6:17).

3. Jesus assures us that God will meet our needs if we trust Him.

"...God will meet all your needs according to his glorious riches in Christ Jesus," Paul wrote to the Philippian church—and to us (Philippians 4:19). Jesus said that God knows what we need even before we ask Him. He cares about the needs of our lives.

A former student of mine named Dawn is a missionary in Central America. She and her family depend on their supporters for the money to meet their financial needs. They have learned to trust God to work in the hearts of individuals to provide for their material well-being. When Dawn and her husband, Bill, were concerned about some expensive repairs needed on their car, they dealt with it— as they always do—in prayer. They simply turned their need over to God. Shortly afterward, they received a check from a supporter for just enough to cover the repairs.

God will meet our needs, but on His terms and in His timing. When we are willing to trust Him fully, not only with the need but also with just how and when the need will be met, we can face life with confidence, security, and freedom.

By contrast, the Bible assures us that no matter how much earthly gain we accumulate, that alone will never satisfy us. We will always live in discontent. "Whoever loves money never has money enough; whoever loves wealth is never satisfied with his income" (Ecclesiastes 5:10).

4. Jesus promises us a life of richness and fullness unrelated to material possessions.

Jesus came to fill our spiritual emptiness. No matter

how full our warehouses become, possessions can never fill our hearts. "A man's life does not consist in the abundance of his possessions," Jesus said (Luke 12:15). Our deepest needs can be filled only when we experience the personal, empowering presence of Christ. Then we enjoy true "prosperity."

This is the prosperity promised in the Old Testament to those who obey God's commandments. This is the ultimate sense of well-being: the knowledge that we are moving toward the goal of being all that God made us to be and that He will give us everything we need to fulfill our potential for Him. We "prosper" in the deepest, richest sense, just as the nation of Israel was "made great" by God. We are "made great" as we experience His infinite power in our daily lives and grow in the knowledge and wisdom of God. That's a true "prosperity theology."

God doesn't forbid us to possess the warehouse and its contents. But He calls us to remain outside its doors, lest we cut ourselves off from the light of His presence by dwelling inside.

Does God want us to be rich or poor? I don't think our material or social success even registers on the scale of what God calls riches. I believe what He wants is for us to be faithful—faithful in commitment, faithful in vision, faithful in stewardship—whether our earthly warehouse contains a great deal or only a little.

— 4 —
Hiding Place #3: Inside the Photo Album

On my desk at work, I have a photo of myself with two dear friends, Cathy and John. It was taken at a picnic on a sunny day. We have our arms around each other, and we're laughing. Looking at the photo, anyone could see that a very special moment of friendship and joy was captured on film.

On top of the filing cabinet, there's another photo, taken when my son was two, after we had been to the beach. He's asleep on his dad's lap, clutching a small starfish in one hand. His father is resting his cheek against the small blond head. There is an indescribable tenderness about the picture that almost brings tears to my eyes every time I look at it.

That's just at the office. At home, I have a whole cupboard full of photo albums and loose snapshots that chronicle my life from my second birthday through last summer's vacation. There are photos of my mother and of my father, who died fifteen years ago; of other relatives, some still living and others dead; of friends I haven't seen in years; wedding pictures (mine and other people's). It's as though these relationships have been frozen in time, to be remembered, savored, re-lived. Browsing through my clutter of photos, I feel a deep sense of richness that *people* give to my life, the important roles so many people have played in my becoming and being who I am.

How about you? Who's in your personal "photo album"? What relationships have shaped your life? Which ones are most important now?

The people around us play a pivotal role in shaping who we are and what we do. Our parents, siblings, and grandparents, our teachers, friends, pastors, our bosses and co-workers, even individuals we meet only in passing but who influence us in some way—all of these people have an impact on our lives. Some of them enrich us, some teach us, some encourage us, some anger us, and some hurt us, but they each have an impact.

Because people are so important to us, we face the temptation to hide inside our personal "photo albums," that is, to hide from God within the security of our human relationships. We look to these relationships to define us, to verify our worth, to set our moral and behavioral standards, instead of learning to trust God for those things.

Let's look into this hiding place and meet some of the individuals who are hiding there.

Hiding on the Home Front.
Ruth is a wife and the mother of four children. She devotes all her time and energy to fulfilling those important roles. She takes pride in the sacrifices she's made for her family. After all, aren't marriage and parenthood God-given responsibilities? She's doing her best to be a model wife and to teach her children right values. Surely, she tells herself, God doesn't expect her to do more than that?

Hiding in the One-Commandment Corner.
Bert's parents were always very strict with him and his brother and sister. Any disobedience was met with punishment. His father was outspoken and opinionated, and his mother pretty much just went along with him. The children learned at an early age not to question anything their father said.

When Bert was in college and began to meet people whose backgrounds and views were very different from his, it made him uncomfortable. He had learned from his father, for example, that people of other cultures, colors, or countries "weren't as good" as "people like us." He had learned that the most important thing in life is to stay ahead of the other guy, no matter what it takes, and never to trust anyone because "they're just out to get you."

Gradually, Bert began to avoid people and ideas that caused him to question his parents' views. It was a lot easier to do that than to reevaluate his whole value system. After all, the Bible says to honor your parents. Who was he to argue with that?

Hiding in the Comfort Zone.
Jan is 26 and single (after a painful divorce two years ago). Her social life revolves around her close-knit group of friends, both men and women, who all went through grade school and high school together. She can't remember a time when "the gang" wasn't a vital part of her life. They have barbecues in the summer and go skating in the winter, and help each other out whenever there's a need. For instance, when Jan's roof started to leak last fall, and she didn't have the money to get it fixed, the group showed up one Saturday with a vanload of supplies and tools and repaired it.

One of the reasons the gang has stayed so close is that

they all have similar backgrounds, having grown up together in the old neighborhood. They share a common set of values and beliefs. Being a part of the group gives her a sense of belonging, a feeling of "rootedness," an assurance that there'll always be someone there when she needs them.

Jan doesn't think much about what God wants of her; she's completely comfortable with the philosophies and standards of the group.

Hiding in the Corner Office.

Bonnie was elated when her boss, the vice-president for financial services, told her she had been chosen to be the new head of the accounting department. She's determined to prove to him that she can be the best director of accounting the company's ever had. She goes home at night and reads books on management and new accounting methods, and outlines new ways to streamline the work of the department.

Bonnie weighs every decision in terms of how it will look to those around her at work. She chooses clothes that look businesslike and authoritative, in keeping with the latest magazine articles on workplace wardrobes; she makes a special effort to be friendly to everyone in the department without seeming to favor one subordinate over another; she makes her lunch plans carefully, working to build a good network of career allies.

Bonnie's the first to admit that right now her career and her job relationships are the most important things in her life, and everything she does is focused on them. After all, doesn't God want us to be successful?

Hiding in the Role-Model Rut.

Joe and his wife, Sandi, visited numerous churches

when they first moved to town seven years ago. They wanted to be sure they found the right church for themselves and their children: a Bible-believing, friendly, family-oriented church that was active in the community. The first time they went to a Sunday morning service at Central Bible Church and heard Rev. Peter Simons preach, they knew they'd found a church home.

Since then, they've continued to marvel at Rev. Simons's incredible leadership ability. Not only does he deliver vibrant, challenging, scripturally sound sermons, but he's also immensely popular with the church family, from the preschoolers to the senior adults. His dynamic personality and seemingly endless supply of energy constantly inspire the congregation to start new programs and to cultivate greater spiritual maturity.

Joe and Sandi feel blessed just to be a part of Rev. Simons's congregation and to know him personally. They rely on his guidance in virtually every area of their lives: parenting, Christian stewardship of their finances, job-related decisions, and their own spiritual growth. Sometimes they wonder what would become of their church and them personally if he accepted a pastorate or a teaching position somewhere else. The very thought of his leaving fills them with panic.

Are Ruth, Bert, Jan and the others deliberately trying to hide from God? I don't think so. It's easy to hide within our personal relationships and not even be aware of it.

Let's look at five basic ways that we work ourselves into this particular kind of hiding place.

1. We derive our identity from other people or from our relationships with them.

Ruth is a good example of this. She has committed all that she is to fulfilling her roles of wife and mother. She defines herself totally in terms of those relationships and has no time for, or interest in, anything else. She's convinced herself that this is what God wants from her at this time in her life.

Desiring to be a good wife and mother certainly isn't wrong; our world could definitely use more women with that desire. But Ruth has things backward. She's telling God what to do instead of seeking what He would have her do. Instead of saying, "God, you've given me this marriage and these children. Show me how these relationships fit into your overall plan for me, and how can I best fulfill these roles in order to glorify you," she's telling Him, "Well, Lord, since I'm a wife and mother, I have my hands full, so don't expect me to worry about anything else until I can at least get these kids through school, okay?"

Earthly relationships, defined by our own parameters, placed ahead of our responsibility to simply be what God calls us to be, interferes with our growth and hinders us from glimpsing the fullness of His vision for us. It also places human limits on His plans to make us unique human beings, each with a special job to do for Him.

By hiding as she is, Ruth leaves herself open to the devastation of losing all her identity and sense of self-worth if something should happen to the relationships to which she's committed herself. A divorce. A fatal accident. A child turning to drugs or running away. Or children simply becoming adults and leaving. How will Ruth view herself then?

2. We establish our values based on what someone else wants or thinks.

On the surface, Bert has it easy. As far as he's concerned, he's inherited a ready-made value system, a set of standards and beliefs handed down intact from his parents to him. He doesn't have to grapple with tough questions about right or wrong or try to understand what God would have him do in any given situation. A complete set of answers has been handed to him.

Bert's disregarding an important reality, though: people can be wrong. By simply adopting his parents' values and attitudes with no questions asked, Bert is buying into whatever human errors may lie within his parents' views. God deals uniquely and individually with each person, and each of us has the responsibility to seek Him on our own.

The Christian life isn't hereditary in an earthly sense. The standards and values that stem from a personal Christian commitment don't get handed down from generation to generation, like Grandma's china, in a neat package. When we "inherit eternal life," we inherit the challenge of living and growing in our unique walk with Jesus Christ as co-heirs of the Father.

3. We rely on other people to meet all our needs.

A sense of belonging is one of the most fundamental human needs. Closely akin to it is our need for emotional security, a feeling that someone cares about us. For Jan, being a part of "the gang" meets those needs. She doesn't need to look any farther than the other members of the group for emotional support.

It's a great blessing to have such good friends. Like many people, I've moved around a lot over the years. Although I made the choice not to stay in my hometown, I sometimes feel a twinge of envy when I meet people who live, as adults, in the hometowns they grew up in, surrounded by lifelong friends and familiar places.

The danger of Jan's hiding place lies in relying on her group of friends to meet all her needs for belonging and self-worth and security. By doing so, she's obscuring her position as a child of God, belonging to Him, relying on Him for those things no human relationship can fulfill.

In addition, by automatically letting her moral, ethical, and behavioral standards be set by the group, Jan, like Bert, is avoiding the important questions about God's personal and individual plan for her and His standards for her life. The group insulates her from seriously considering what God expects. God's standards are perfect; they are unchanging, and they are designed to bring about the very best for us. Can we honestly say the same of human standards?

4. We construct an artificial set of values and substitute them for God's.

Bonnie has worked hard to attain her new position. No wonder she's excited and preoccupied; she feels that at last all her training and hard work have paid off.

When we find ourselves in a new job situation, it's natural to want to prove ourselves. Bonnie, however, is allowing her career role to shape her whole value system. She's letting her job goals and relationships shape every decision she makes, from how she dresses to who her friends are. God's values are crowded out by the values of the corporate environment.

Everything in Bonnie's environment supports her success-oriented value system. The company she works for rewards initiative and hard work. The media reinforce the drive for success and create glowing images of successful men and women. The world applauds those who are able to succeed in business.

Anyone who's been in the business world knows that there is such a thing as the "corporate culture"—a specific, largely unwritten set of values and standards govern any business or organization. This culture dictates the basis of decision-making, the codes of conduct—both official and unofficial—and even the way relationships are cultivated, formed, and maintained.

The weakness of those rules, though, is that they're all man-made. They may—but probably don't!—reflect Christian standards and principles.

The Apostle Paul warns us about buying into earthly value systems. "See to it that no one takes you captive through hollow and deceptive philosophy, which depends on human tradition and the basic principles of this world rather than on Christ" (Colossians 2:8). False value systems aren't just those preached by offbeat religious gurus or lunatic-fringe cults. The most dangerous ones, in reality, are the ones that are most plausible. Like the unspoken "rules of the game" within any company.

Being a conscientious and hard-working employee, like Bonnie, is commendable, not a cause for criticism. The danger of playing the corporate game too seriously, though, is that we may begin to feel that those rules are more important than God's rules. And that's what's happened to Bonnie.

For example, Bonnie is working hard to please her supervisor, the vice-president. What if he asks her to do something she doesn't feel is ethically or morally right? Will she be willing to stand up to him, or will she choose to adjust her own standards to accommodate his? How far will she be willing to compromise?

What about these "useful" friendships she's cultivating with people who can help her move up the career ladder? Will she grow so accustomed to relationships based on what others can do for her that she'll forget how to have a real friendship based on common interests, mutual respect, and affection?

As a department head, she'll have a whole staff to manage. In her drive to make them a productive and efficient department, will she lose sight of individual staff members' needs for recognition, reassurance, and encouragement? When a staff member has a personal problem that affects his or her work, will Bonnie be able to handle the situation with compassion and sensitivity, or will her only concern be maintaining the department's output until the staff member can get "squared away"?

In all her striving to be the perfect "company woman," will Bonnie lose sight of who God wants her to be, what He expects of her? Will she maintain an open, godly testimony to those around her—without respect to who they are or what they can do for her career?

When our photo album becomes filled with pictures of us in our work roles, and we allow those images to define us completely, then it becomes easy for God's commandments and His values to get lost among all the competition. The Holy Spirit's still, small voice is easily drowned out by the beat of the corporate drumroll, if we're tuned in to it alone.

5. We ascribe to human beings the authority we should reserve for God.

Joe and Sandi are fortunate to have found a church home that meets their needs. To have a pastor who provides sound biblical preaching, dynamic leadership, and genuine personal concern for individual church members is a blessing indeed.

That's how my friend Suzanne felt about her pastor. She admired him in every aspect of life. She held his spiritual insight in such high esteem that she believed anything he said was truly in keeping with God's Word and His will. To her, he was the model of a man of God.

Suzanne's entire church was plunged into chaos when it was revealed that the pastor was having an extramarital affair with a woman who had come to him for counseling. This man—a visionary leader and spiritual guide to a congregation of several thousand people—was shown to be subject to the same weaknesses as the rest of us.

Suzanne was devastated. She cried everytime she thought about the "fall" of her pastor. "I feel like I'll never look up to anyone again," she told me brokenheartedly. "My trust and respect have been so totally betrayed. How can I ever believe again that a person is what he seems to be?"

As her admiration for her pastor had grown, Suzanne had lost sight of the fact that he was just a man, a human being subject to all the frailties of the sinful nature. Being a Christian—even a minister—doesn't remove us from the world's temptations; it just gives us the capability to resist them. But that capability is still limited by our own degree of surrender and our humanness.

When, like Joe and Sandi and Suzanne, we encounter someone who becomes a role model for us, we need to remember that he or she is still human. We can learn from them, be enriched by them, emulate the aspects of their lives that are most godly. Yet, we must reserve our reliance and reverence for God. If our spiritual welfare is founded on the teachings and the model of anyone other than Christ—even someone committed to Him—the foundation is quicksand.

The Apostle Paul warned the Christians at Corinth against this very danger, when some of them began to describe themselves as followers of individual evangelists, including himself. "What, after all, is Apollos? And what is Paul? Only servants, through whom you came to believe—as the Lord has assigned to each his task. I planted the seed, Apollos watered it, but God made it grow. So neither he who plants nor he who waters it is anything, but only God, who makes things grow" (I Corinthians 3: 5-7).

Feeling Halved, Being Whole

Sara's husband died last spring of lung cancer, leaving her to rear their two small children alone. Just a short time before her husband received his bleak prognosis, she had scheduled an appointment at a photographer's studio for a family portrait. She dressed the children in their Sunday-best, and the whole family trooped off to the studio. Now, after a year of adjustment and struggle, she looks at the framed 8"x10" photo on her dresser and she can hardly remember what life was like back then. Was it all a dream, or was there really a time when her family was intact, when she felt a sense of wholeness?

Sara's marriage was, as she puts it, "one of the all-time great ones." She and her husband were not only spouses and lovers, but the best of friends. "I feel like half a person now," she said right after he died, "not a whole. I go around with this overwhelming sense that a huge part of me is missing. I need to find a totally new way of seeing myself and my family."

God calls us to wholeness, to completeness in Him apart from our day-to-day roles. As we've seen, human relationships are subject to the realities of death, distance, change, and a whole host of other elements that can sever or damage the relationship. To let ourselves be defined by such impermanent circumstances is to create a fragile self-image that may not survive the inevitable changes life brings.

Human relationships are subject to another set of forces, too: the evils of the sinful nature. Suzanne saw in her pastor's life what happens when Satan gets the upper hand, even temporarily. The old nature surfaces in less public but equally painful ways in our day-to-day interactions, too. A co-worker becomes jealous when we receive praise or credit for good work. A friend becomes angry when we disagree about an important moral or political issue. A spouse reacts with sarcasm and barbs of criticism when we try to explain that he or she has hurt us. A longtime neighbor stops speaking to us after a misunderstanding about repairing a fence.

Human relationships are fraught with misunderstanding, miscommunication, and cross-purposes. People say things without thinking. They criticize others without knowing all the facts. They become jealous over the accomplishments or material possessions of others and angry when they feel threatened or challenged. They focus on their own needs and desires while stomping roughshod over the feelings of others. They put their will before God's and before other people's. They choose their relationships based on physical attraction or temporary emotional needs or career expedience, and then move on when the purpose has been served.

Human beings aren't a very good foundation for our most basic emotional and spiritual needs. We are all susceptible to attitudes, motivations, and behavior that stem from our sinful nature. The Apostle Paul lists a whole catalog of unpleasant qualities that sin visits on us (from Galatians 5:19-20):

sexual immorality	impurity
debauchery	idolatry
witchcraft	discord
hatred	fits of rage
jealousy	dissensions
selfish ambition	envy
factions	orgies
drunkenness	"and the like"

While these qualities wreak havoc in our daily lives on an individual basis, we have only to read the newspaper to see large-scale evidence of sin and Satan at work. Racial conflict. Power struggles within and between countries. Random killings. Drug-related robberies and murders. Domestic violence. Sexual abuse.

Fortunately, God gives us the power, through the Holy Spirit, to overcome our sinful nature and to transform our thinking and behavior. But, because we are imperfect, we often slip. Satan is always there, lurking, waiting to create chaos in our relationships as well as our testimonies.

Even people who love us and care about us—our spouses, children, parents, siblings, friends—occasionally cause us pain. They hurt, misunderstand, anger or become angry with us. Much of the time, it's not that they want or intend to do those things; it's just that they're human, too. When we accept their humanity, and at the same time accept our own, we become free to savor our relationships without the baggage of misplaced dependency and unrealistic expectations.

Meet Ray, who learned a hard lesson about expectations and human frailty.

Ray had loved and admired his father for as long as he could remember. His father, Richard, was self-employed as an appliance repairman. In his earliest childhood memories, Ray always pictured his dad fixing things: tinkering with this or that around the house, miraculously repairing the bicycle with the broken chain or the airconditioner that blew out hot air or the kitchen faucet that went drip. . .drip. . .drip all night long.

"My dad can do anything!" Ray would tell his friends.

When Ray's dad wasn't fixing things or at work, he was throwing grounders for Ray to catch or planning a fishing expedition at the lake. Superman, who even had his own TV show, was only second best in Ray's mind.

When Ray was in high school, he began to notice that his

father seemed to be drinking quite a bit in the evenings after he came home from work. He'd become loud and have trouble controlling his temper. Ray tried to understand. He attributed his father's behavior to the pressures of running a business and raising a family, and he tried hard to do all the right things so that he wouldn't upset his father.

Eventually Ray got married and moved into a home not far from his parents'. One night he received a frantic call from his mother. "Your father has had a car accident and been arrested for drunk driving. I'm scared to death that he'll have to go to jail. Ray, he's in serious trouble. I just don't know what to do."

Ray was dumbfounded. He knew his dad had been drinking a little more over the past several years, but a drunk driver? He couldn't believe it. There must be a mistake.

Ray's father didn't have to serve a jail sentence, but his driver's license was suspended for two years. He was fined $10,000, which he had to borrow. He was required to perform 100 hours of community service and attend a safe-driving school. And he was ordered to enroll in a year-long counseling program for alcoholics.

When Ray's mother told him all this, he hit the ceiling. "Counseling program for alcoholics?" he repeated in disbelief. "What are those people thinking? Dad's not an alcoholic!"

Ray's mother looked at him sadly. "Of course he is, Ray," she said. "Your dad's drinking problem has just gotten steadily worse over the last ten years or so. You didn't see it because you didn't want to. I'm sorry you had to end up facing it this way."

For weeks after that, Ray just couldn't face his dad. He always found excuses to avoid going to his parents' for dinner and managed to be "busy" when his dad invited him to a ball game.

Finally, after several months, Ray's mother called him at work. "Ray, you can't avoid your father for the rest of your life," she told him. "He's a human being, weak and fallible like everyone else, and he's made a terrible mistake. Can't you just accept him as he is?"

"No, I can't," Ray answered bitterly. "Look, Mom, you and I both know someone could have been killed in that accident. Dad could have crippled a child for life or seriously hurt someone. What kind of person takes a chance like that?

"All my life, everything I've done was to please Dad and to be like him. School, sports, hobbies, everything. I did it all for him. And now I find out he wasn't who I thought he was at all. I feel betrayed. I don't know if I ever want to see him again."

After he hung up the phone, Ray looked at a photo sitting on his desk. It showed his dad and him in fishing gear, each holding up a 2" minnow and grinning mischievously at the camera.

Ray dropped it into the wastebasket.

Ray just couldn't accept his father's human weakness. Ray had built his life's structure around his dad's example, and now he felt as though that structure had been torn down around him. All the needs his father had met for him—security, identity, values—were now in limbo, were needs in search of a way to be met.

What a perfect setting to learn reliance on God, along with trust, faith, and forgiveness.

Does Ray have to stop loving his father? Does he have to stop believing his father did his best all those years? Does he have to write his father off as a failure, a poor human being, a phony? Of course not. Nor does Ray have to approve or excuse what his father has done or will do in the future. Ray only has to acknowledge that his father is human—just as he himself is—and prone to weaknesses. Then he can love and accept him on that basis. Once he does that, his relationship can be restored, built on a foundation of love and *reality* that will endure the strains of daily life.

Standing on the Rock

God promises to meet our needs. When we accept His sovereignty in our lives, and turn our focus away from human beings, we can live with confidence, assured that He is as constant as humans are uncertain.

In the same way that God promises to meet our material needs, He also promises to meet our whole range of emotional and spiritual needs. Once we decide to rely on Him, we put an end to the frustrating exercise of demanding that other people meet these needs for us. We can stop trying to hide in our photo albums.

The psalmist describes the many ways God stands ready to meet our needs:

> "Praise the Lord, O my soul,
> and forget not all his benefits—
> [He] forgives all your sins
> and heals all your diseases,
> [He] redeems your life from the pit
> and crowns you with love and compassion,
> [He] satisfies your desires with good things
> so that your youth is renewed like the eagle's. . . .
> The Lord is compassionate and gracious,
> slow to anger, abounding in love.
> He will not always accuse,
> nor will he harbor his anger forever;

> he does not treat us as our sins deserve
> or repay us according to our iniquities. . . .
> As far as the east is from the west,
> so far has he removed our transgressions from us.
> As a father has compassion on his children,
> so the Lord has compassion on those who fear him;
> for he knows how we are formed,
> he remembers that we are dust. . . .
> But from everlasting to everlasting
> the Lord's love is with those who fear him.
> Praise the Lord, O my soul."
> (Psalm 103:2-5,8-9,12-14,17,19b)

Let's examine some of these needs God promises to meet:

—*The Need to be Forgiven*—

If we had to carry around the accumulated burden of a lifetime's sins and wrongdoing, the weight of them would break us spiritually and emotionally. Forgiveness renews us; it gives us the opportunity to start over, to grow in faithfulness free of past mistakes. "He will not always accuse, nor will he harbor his anger forever" (Psalm 103:9). "If we confess our sins, he is faithful and just and will forgive us our sins and purify us from all unrighteousness" (I John 1:9).

God's forgiveness is perfect and complete. People, on the other hand, "forgive and forget" on a far more limited basis. We often have long memories when it comes to hurts inflicted by others. We may sincerely want to forgive, but we find it hard to forget. Only as we grow in God's grace and give freer and freer reign to His Spirit within us can we come close to His kind of forgiveness. Only then do we learn both to forgive ourselves and to love others in a way that "keeps no record of wrongs" (I Corinthians 13:5).

—The Need for Healing—

Men and women are subject to so many diseases of the heart and spirit: anger, despair, self-hate, bitterness, aloneness, alienation, aimlessness; the list goes on. God wants to heal us, to make us well. If we let Him, He promises to repair the wounds caused by torn relationships or unrealized hopes or unsatisfied desires, to strengthen and nurture our ailing spirits with a new sense of value and purpose and optimism. When we hurt, He heals.

—The Need for Self-Worth—

Jesus Christ paid for our sins. Through His sacrificial and vicarious death and atonement, He bought us back from the pit of eternal death. When we doubt our own value, when we feel that we are failures or that we are just tiny cogs in a big meaningless world, we have lost sight of the ultimate price God placed on us, our souls, and our salvation.

In the everyday world, people often value us only for what they feel we can give them. But God values us simply because we are His. What more do we need to convince us that we are worthwhile?

—The Need for Caring—

If you look back on your school years, does one teacher stand out in your mind as the best teacher you ever had? Or the most interested in seeing you succeed? If so, I'll bet the one thing you remember best about that teacher was that he or she truly cared about you. In the county where I live, the schools have a "Teacher of the Year" Award. Invariably, when the finalists and, ultimately, the winner are announced, they are described as teachers who genuinely care about students' needs and their welfare. These are teachers who sincerely share in their students' ups and downs; they rejoice in every student's accomplishments and encourage in the face of every shortcoming. They are caring, and they are compassionate.

It's a fact of human existence that we need to have people care about us. We need to feel that it matters to *someone* what happens to us and how our life is going. Compassion is a special kind of caring; it's an active, genuine empathy that involves us in the needs, feelings, and desires of others. Their concerns become our concerns. Our friend Jan, whom we met earlier, felt this kind of caring and compassion from her group of friends.

God is not only caring, He is also compassionate. His care isn't an objective desire to see that our needs are met, but a passionate—and compassionate—desire to give us His very best. At any given time in our lives, whether we are traveling peaks or valleys, He is with us, sharing victories and burdens alike. People, on the other hand, pick and choose when to stick by us and when to steer clear. They may be there for us to depend on in one period of our lives, and then be conspicuously absent during another. Only God is always faithful. "Never will I leave you; never will I forsake you" (Hebrews 13:5).

—The Need for Patience—

God is "slow to anger." "He knows how we are formed." God knows we are human, not divine. He recognizes our faults, tolerates our weaknesses, and forgives our misdeeds, only to see us repeat them—and He forgives us again each time we ask. He doesn't hold our mistakes against us, storing them up like an ugly collection of junk;

instead, He patiently waits for us to grow in faithfulness and obedience under His loving eye. Unlike human beings, who may grow exasperated or run out of patience with us, God never gives up on us (John 14:16-17,23).

—*The Need for Acceptance*—

Yesterday at work we had a surprise bridal shower for Susie, a data entry clerk in our department. After she had opened all her gifts and we had shared the punch and cookies, she said tearfully, "This is the nicest thing anyone's ever done for me. You all have been so generous; thank you so much."

Susie is one of those co-workers whom everyone loves. She's kind, thoughtful, and helpful; her gentle and loving spirit is always evident to anyone who happens to be around. As the shower demonstrated, she's a person who makes others *want* to be generous toward her.

God's generosity toward us is different. "But God demonstrates his own love for us in this: While we were still sinners, Christ died for us" (Romans 5:8). God isn't generous to us because we deserve it or because, like Susie, we are such nice people. He is generous to us because He accepts us *as we are, in spite of* the way we are, in spite of our sins and weaknesses. He is generous to us simply because He loves us and we are His children. As the psalmist says, "He does not treat as our sins deserve" (Psalm 103:10a); instead, He "satisfies your desires with good things" (vs. 5)—including His love, forgiveness, a sense of worth, patience—and wholeness.

If I'm whole, why do I need you?

Wholeness doesn't mean isolation. Learning to see ourselves as whole through God's empowering love isn't a way of telling other people, "Stay away from me; I don't need anyone else." Human relationships give us a feeling of connectedness with the world around us; they give us the special moments of shared joy, shared laughter, and even shared pain that confirm our sense of belonging to the human race. As an old folk saying goes, "Friendship divides sorrow and doubles joy."

God calls us to unity in marriage, to responsibility in parenthood, to fellowship within the Christian community. He calls us to honor and respect within the family and to loving servanthood to all mankind. He often uses other people to accomplish His work in our lives as they love us, nurture us, teach us, challenge us—and even make our lives miserable! But above all, He calls us to wholeness in Him. It is our relationship to Him that defines us, not our relationship to other human beings.

"You are mine; I am yours."

The Bible reassures us that we always have an identity, a rich parental inheritance—from God—and a Friend we can count on, no matter how dark the skies or how deep the valley. Whether our earthly relationships meet our needs or not, these things are ours. Whether or not our loved ones understand or forgive or care about us, Christ cares. Whether people meet our expectations or let us down again and again, God is on our side.

> "As the Father has loved me, so have I loved you. Now remain in my love. If you obey my commands, you will remain in my love, just as I have obeyed my Father's commands and remain in his love. . . .Greater love has no one than this, that he lay down his life for his friends. You are my friends if you do what I command. I no longer call you servants, because a servant does not

know his master's business. Instead, I have called you friends, for everything that I learned from my Father I have made known to you. You did not choose me, but I chose you to go and bear fruit—fruit that will last. . . .This is my command: Love each other" (John 15:9-10,13-17).

The Cost of Belonging

Jesus preached some strong words about human relationships *vs.* our relationship with Him.

The Gospel of Matthew records this incident, which also appears in Mark and Luke:

"While Jesus was still talking to the crowd, his mother and brothers stood outside, wanting to speak to him. Someone told him, 'Your mother and brothers are standing outside, wanting to speak to you.'

"He replied to him, 'Who is my mother, and who are my brothers?' Pointing to his disciples, he said, 'Here are my mother and my brothers. For whoever does the will of my Father in heaven is my brother and sister and mother.' " (12:46-50).

In another passage, Jesus spoke of family relationships:

"Large crowds were traveling with Jesus, and turning to them he said, 'If anyone comes to me and does not hate his father and mother, his wife and children, his brothers and sisters—yes, even his own life—he cannot be my disciple. And anyone who does not carry his cross and follow me cannot be my disciple'" (Luke 14:25-27).

Whoa! Wait a minute.

Hate our parents? Hate our children? Hate our lives? What is Jesus telling us here? What about God's commands to honor our parents, to rear our children in the nurture and admonition of the Lord, to know the blessings God wants for us?

These passages are not about hating our family members or disregarding our relationships or going through our lives in misery. They are about priorities.

Let's review the story of a well-known biblical character whom God taught a dramatic lesson about the priority placed on human relationships. The Bible tells us:

"Some time later God tested Abraham. He said to him, 'Abraham!'

" 'Here I am,' he replied.

"Then God said, 'Take your son, your only son, Isaac, whom you love, and go to the region of Moriah. Sacrifice him there as a burnt offering on one of the mountains I will tell you about' " (Genesis 22:1-2).

Abraham obeyed. He saddled his donkey, gathered wood, made sure he had his knife with him, and set out for the mountains. Imagine how his heart must have been wrenched when his son asked, "Where is the lamb for the burnt offering?" (Genesis 22:7).

This was Abraham's only child, the son of his old age, the promised blessing from God to him and his beloved wife, Sarah. After a lifetime of walking with God, was this God's "reward"? Abraham was being asked to make a supreme sacrifice, to give up this long-awaited relationship that had brought him such joy.

But he obeyed.

"When they reached the place God had told him about, Abraham built an altar there and arranged the wood on it. He bound his son Isaac and laid him on the altar, on top of the wood. Then he reached out his hand and took the knife to slay his son. But, the angel of the Lord called out to him from heaven, 'Abraham! Abraham!'

" 'Here I am,' he replied.

" 'Do not lay a hand on the boy,' he said. 'Do not do anything to him. Now I know that you fear God, because you have not withheld from me your son, your only son.'" (Genesis 22:9-12).

Abraham loved his son. He treasured the gift of that child. But his priority was to obey God.

Where are your priorities? In the previous chapter, we talked about the fact that God doesn't need our money; it's our willingness to give it back to him that matters. Similarly, when God called Abraham to sacrifice his son, it wasn't the lifeless body of a young boy that He wanted. It was uncomplaining obedience. Commitment. Priority. And Abraham proved what his priority was.

As we look back at Jesus' words in Luke, we see the same theme. It isn't that God wants us to hate our families or despise our friends. He just wants our priorities to be straight. He wants us to put Him first.

When we make that commitment, our human relationships aren't diminished. Instead, they take on new meaning, new depths. They become vehicles for Christian growth, gardens where we can cultivate the fruits of the Spirit. We learn to love others with God's unconditional love...to care about others with Christ's infinite compassion...to reach out to others in the power of the Holy Spirit. We grow more deeply grateful for the blessings of family and friends and the lessons learned from casual acquaintances when we do.

In short, that's when our photo albums become filled to overflowing—as they chronicle the adventure we're living ...for Christ.

— 5 —

Hiding Place #4: Inside the Trophy Case

I'm a Winner!
My neighbor, Peter, has been an athlete all his life. Over the years he has collected an impressive array of trophies, award plaques, and medals which he displays in various places in his home.

A few years ago I traveled with a business associate to a convention in another part of the state. During the five-hour car trip, we talked about countless subjects ranging from global to trivial. In the course of the conversation I lamented, half-kidding, that while my neighbor had shelves and shelves of trophies, I didn't have a single one. Never having been an athlete or a competitor myself, I'd never received one. "Just once," I told my friend, "I'd like to receive a trophy for something!" Then the conversation meandered on to another topic and I didn't give it another thought.

On the way back from the convention, we stopped at a restaurant for some dinner. I knew my friend was tired, so I volunteered to drive. I hadn't driven a stick shift for several years, but I was confident that the knack would come back easily.

Unfortunately, however, the driveway out of the

restaurant's parking lot sloped up sharply toward the street. When I took my foot off the brake to make my turn onto the street, I felt the car begin to roll backward. Overreacting, I floored the accelerator and shot out into the street, nearly knocking over a row of mailboxes while my startled passenger dissolved into laughter. "Boy, I'll bet you laid a patch of rubber in that driveway!" he howled. It took five hours to drive home, and I think maybe he stopped laughing after about three.

A week later a package arrived at my office. Opening it, I discovered inside a foot-high trophy with a shiny model car on the top. The plaque on the front read, "Tire Patch Laying Contest—First Place."

God Doesn't Give Awards—Just Rewards

While winning a trophy for tire-patch laying probably isn't everyone's lifelong dream, in general we all like to receive honor and recognition. It feels good when a supervisor or co-worker says, "Good job." Receiving a bonus for exceptional performance on the job assures us our hard work has been worthwhile. When we work long hours for civic clubs or service organizations, we like to have someone acknowledge it and recognize us for our efforts. Best of all, we like to hear our friends and loved ones say "Thanks" when we've gone out of our way to do something for them.

Our paycheck is a form of recognition, too. It rewards us for doing our jobs satisfactorily. It puts a universally-acknowledged measure of value on what we do.

Recognition reaffirms our self-worth. It tells us what we do is important to someone else. It meets our basic human need to feel appreciated.

Recognition, praise, awards, and honors can make it tempting to try to hide from God amid our own successes, our own accomplishments—in our jobs, our homes, our churches. After all, if we're doing so well on our own, why do we need Him? If we can accomplish so much by ourselves, surely we don't need to complicate our lives with all His rules. Isn't relying on God more for people who don't have a lot going for them, who need help just to make it from day to day?

Brenda was in her mid-twenties, a bright, capable assistant editor of a small magazine. She was very good at her job and had already become recognized in publishing circles as someone with a bright future. She had a strong sense of accomplishment and self-worth and took a great deal of pride in each new issue of the magazine.

Brenda didn't need God to give her a sense of importance or to guide her in making a success of herself. She was doing fine! It was easy to hide from God in her office, surrounded by visible, tangible evidence of her skill and hard work—"trophies" of human applause that attested to her abilities.

When Brenda and her husband decided to start a family, though, she wanted to take some time off from her job so she could spend the baby's first few years at home. And, the idea of a break from the hectic pace of the office sounded kind of appealing.

The baby arrived, a healthy, vigorous boy. Brenda delighted in each tiny step in the baby's development. She dove into motherhood with the same energy she had always put into her job. Before long, though, she began to notice there was a big difference: no one recognized her efforts at being a mother. Day after day she changed diapers, filled baby bottles, aimed spoonsful of pureed beans at a constantly moving target, washed the same tiny garments over and over—and no one said, "Gee, Brenda, nice work."

As the months went by, Brenda's self-esteem dropped lower and lower. When her husband arrived home at the end of the day, she would say, "I don't feel like I've accomplished anything today. I just did all the same things I did yesterday. I do all these things, all this work, and there's nothing to show for it. I feel worthless."

When the baby was several months old, Brenda noticed she felt tired all the time. She had trouble getting up in the morning; she wanted to nap during the day, and went to bed early. She had frequent headaches and her stomach seemed to have become temperamental.

When her doctor examined her, he couldn't find any physical cause for the symptoms she was experiencing. He asked her what was going on in her life. She told him about the baby, about quitting her job, about the way she felt about herself. His diagnosis? Depression. Her physical problems were the result of her negative and unhappy feelings about herself and her day-to-day life.

Brenda had been hiding from God for too long, relying on her professional achievements, her talents, and her job to give her a sense of importance and self-worth. For her, the only worthwhile challenges in life were putting out a better magazine, finding more efficient ways to do things, reaching a higher status in her field. Other aspects of her life were secondary in importance. When she quit her job, suddenly her "trophy case" disappeared, and she no longer had those challenges—or the accomplishments and applause they produced—to support her sense of value, of her contribution to the world.

When we try to hide from God inside our own private "trophy case," whatever form that may take, we run two risks:

First, we run the risk of relying too heavily on our outward achievements to sustain our sense of self-worth.

As a result, if circumstances change and we no longer have those supports holding us up, we feel the bottom has dropped out of our lives and we can't cope.

The second risk is that we begin to overestimate our own power, our own resources, our own abilities. We begin to take credit for things that, in reality, we have achieved only because God has chosen to let us and because He has given us the wherewithal to achieve them.

Let's take a look at how we can come out from behind all those trophies.

1. Recognize that our self-worth is not defined by what we do.

Rev. Joe McLaren used to be on the staff of my home church. A few years ago, he suffered a very serious back injury and had to have major surgery, which was followed by a long and painful period of recuperation. An active, energetic man in his late thirties, Joe is a "doer" if ever there was one.

Joe was gone from the church for many months, during which time he was unable to do anything but lie on his back. We missed him greatly. It was a joyful day for our congregation when he came back and preached his first sermon.

"During my recuperation," Joe said in his sermon, "my self-esteem went lower and lower. I wasn't *doing* anything! I had always gotten my sense of self-worth from the things I did, from being active and accomplishing things. And there I was for all those months, unable even to hold my baby daughter. My family had to wait on me and help me with everything. I felt worthless.

"But you know, everyday while I was in the hospital and after I went home, I received stacks of cards and letters. People wished me a good recovery, said they were praying for me, and told me they missed me. I couldn't believe the number of cards that just kept coming. That outpouring of love and support astonished me. After all, I wasn't *doing* anything to earn it!

"Finally I began to understand that all those people loved me because of who I was, not what I did. Even when I wasn't able to do anything, for myself or anyone else, they still loved me. I still want to do lots of things, but I know now that my self-worth isn't tied to doing them. It's the being that matters. It's who you are, not what you do."

So Who Are You?

If we're to seek our self-worth in who we are rather than what we do, we need to be able to answer the question, "Who am I?" What we do is obvious; we can see physical actions and their results all around us. Defining who we are is more difficult, which is probably why we're so willing to avoid it if we can. Yet, if we examine God's Word to learn who we are, we'll find our true identity:

"Yet to all who received him, to those who believed in his name, he gave the right to become children of God" (John 1:12).

That's who we are: children of God. Once we recognize that loving Father-child relationship, all other "identities" become irrelevant, because we have determined our fundamental identity in God's scheme of things. What we do or don't achieve in life doesn't affect who we are, because we have accepted a complete separation between being and doing.

According to the Bible, our identity as God's children has many facets. As a result of our sonship:

We are stewards over the earth.
"Then God said, 'Let us make man in our own image, in our likeness, and let them rule over the

fish of the sea and the birds of the air, over the livestock, over all the earth, and over all the creatures that move along the ground.' . . .Fill the earth and subdue it" (Genesis 1:26-28).

We are God's most beloved creatures.

"What is man that you are mindful of him, the son of man that you care for him? You made him a little lower than the angels; you crowned him with glory and honor and put everything under his feet" (Hebrews 2:6-8 *cf.* Psalm 8:4-6).

We are gifted in individual and special ways.

"There are different kinds of gifts, but the same Spirit. There are different kinds of service, but the same Lord. There are different kinds of working but the same God works all of them in men.....Now you are the body of Christ and each one of you is a part of it" (I Corinthians 12:4-6,27).

We are keepers of sacred things.

"So then, men ought to regard us as servants of Christ and as those entrusted with the secret things of God" (I Corinthians 4:1).

We are a blessed people.

"Blessed is the nation whose God is the Lord, the people he chose for his inheritance" (Psalm 33:12). "Praise be to the God and Father of our Lord Jesus Christ, who has blessed us. . .with every spiritual blessing in Christ. For he chose us in him before the creation of the world to be holy and blameless in his sight" (Ephesians 1:3-4).

We are victors.

"The Lord is with me; he is my helper. I will look

in triumph on my enemies" (Psalm 118:7). "In all these things we are more than conquerors through him who loved us" (Romans 8:37).

Do people with those kind of credentials really need to rely on their jobs, their roles, or their human awards to be important?

Of course, we are to be "doers," too—doers of the things God's Word instructs us to do (James 1-2). But our inherent value and our place in this world are ours *before* the doing. We are important because we are God's. The being comes first; the doing follows after.

The world's way is just the opposite. To get the world's approval, we have to *do* things first: perform our jobs well, devote ourselves to community service, outshine others in competition, be outstanding parents, employees, students, citizens. Only by doing can we prove that we are valuable. That's a sad situation, and it creates a lot of stress and pressure. If we buy into it, we *have* to measure ourselves by the world's standards of accomplishment. Brenda learned firsthand the dangers of that. What a relief to know that God loves us because of who we are, not what we do.

2. Avoid the pitfall of trying to earn God's approval.

We grow so accustomed to striving for recognition, rewards, approval, and acceptance that we often try, intentionally or not, to apply that same principle of cause-and-effect to our spiritual lives. We reason that if we do certain things, we'll win God's favor.

The problem with this doing-oriented approach is that in the flurry of activity we can lose sight of what it means to simply be a child of God. We begin to rely on our good deeds to give us the feeling of being "right" with God. When that happens, we feel little need for faith and commitment. In short, like our friend Irene in Chapter 1, we hide behind a barrier of our "religious" activities, trying to "buy" righteousness like the Pharisees.

We know what God wants us to *do* in our daily lives—be actively concerned about the needs of others, take a stand for righteousness, show respect and faithfulness to the things of God. But these actions are the outward demonstrations of our identity in God, not the source of it.

Think about this: who is the oldest person you know? Perhaps a family member or an acquaintance in the community who has lived to be 98 or 100 or maybe 102 years old? Maybe you've read about this person in the newspaper even if he or she isn't known to you personally.

Now, how many of these individuals who have lived such exceptionally long lives would be able to take the church youth group on a camping trip? Drive the church bus? Could they wield a hammer and saw and do the needed repairs to the fellowship hall? Supervise 15 or 20 active toddlers in the church nursery? Organize and carry out an annual fund drive?

Realistically speaking, probably not. These individuals have probably experienced poor health or are limited in their ability to get around. Maybe their sight or hearing is impaired. Perhaps they are even bedridden. Are they automatically, then, unable to please God because they can't be out doing the things that need to be done in the world?

Of course not. Elderly Christians who have lived long lives of faithfulness know with certainty that their favor with God is the result of His grace, not their deeds. They don't need to prove their worth to Him or strive to earn His love. There is a great deal we can learn from long-experienced servants of God who have found the secret of a peaceful spirit.

3. Keep our accomplishments in perspective.

I had a sick feeling in my heart recently when I read a magazine interview with one of our country's "fallen" evangelists. The man was saying in the interview that he was confident that he would overcome the trials brought on by his public disgrace and that he would rebuild his ministry and prosper again. The interview concluded with this quote: "I'm going to save more souls than ever."

This man had forgotten an important fact about evangelism: men and women do not save souls; God does. Somehow he had lost his perspective on the relative roles that he and God played in the work of salvation.

God gives success. We can only be His channel.

This principle applies not just to TV evangelists but to all of us, whatever our work may be. When Nehemiah and his companions set out to rebuild the wall at Jerusalem, they were surrounded by enemies. Hostile leaders and armies tried deception, sabotage, and outright attack to keep the builders from succeeding. Yet in 52 days the wall was completed.

Nehemiah had succeeded. His exemplary leadership, his careful planning, his dedication and hard work all paid off. Nehemiah was to go down in history as a man of vision and action, a leader who still inspires us today.

But when the wall was completed, Nehemiah didn't claim the credit. He reported it this way:

"So the wall was completed. . . . When all our enemies heard about this, all the surrounding nations were afraid and lost their self-confidence, because they realized that this work had been done with the help of our God" (Nehemiah 6:15).

Throughout the rebuilding, Nehemiah's reliance had been on God, not on his own abilities. He constantly sought God's favor, guidance, and help—and he remembered to thank God for every success. Nowhere in the story of Nehemiah is there any indication that he gave himself credit for the success of his effort.

Everything we have and are comes from God. Mental and physical abilities; the capacity to learn, to master skills, to develop talents; the material resources to make things happen; the circumstances that allow us to achieve. Without these blessings from God, we could do nothing.

Certainly Brenda would not have been able to attain her level of achievement without God-given abilities, a suitable job environment, good health, and life itself. To take credit for our accomplishments as though we attained them solely on our own is to deny God's claim on our lives.

This doesn't mean that nothing we do is important; God cherishes us too much for that. In fact, just the opposite is true: everything we do is important to Him. The Bible tells us that "from his dwelling place he watches all who live on earth—he who forms the hearts of all, who considers everything they do" (Psalm 33:15).

When our lives are consecrated to God, He wants us to be successful—to honor Him—in the things we undertake. How we do our jobs is important to Him. How we rear our children, treat our parents, interact with our friends and co-workers, participate in our community—all these things are important to God. He made us. He created us with the capacity to be and do more than we, with our limited vision and insight, can imagine. He alone knows our potential, because He created it. When we seek His will in our efforts, and then His blessing, then we are at our best. And when we perform to the very best of our God-given ability, eventually the world will notice, too. Maybe we'll even receive a trophy. But best of all, our efforts will be pleasing to God.

"Therefore judge nothing before the appointed

time; wait until the Lord comes. He will bring to light what is hidden in darkness and will expose the motives of men's hearts. At that time each will receive his praise from God" (I Corinthians 4:5).
Praise from God.
Imagine what it will feel like to receive praise from God. All the world's forms of recognition pale by comparison.

— 6 —

Hiding Place #5: Outside the Voting Booth

Several weeks before the last presidential election, I happened to run into Howard, a man I knew casually through a mutual friend. Just making conversation, I asked Howard whom he planned to vote for in the election.

"I don't know yet," he said. "I'm kind of waiting to learn more about the candidates as the campaign goes on. I don't feel like I have enough information yet."

A couple of weeks later, I saw Howard at a party. We began to talk about the presidential campaign again. Howard still hadn't made up his mind how to vote but was giving it a great deal of thought and consideration. As we talked about the pros and cons of the two candidates, I was astounded at the amount of information Howard had read and listened to in his effort to select the best candidate. He referred to a half-dozen news magazines, several newspapers, and numerous television commentaries. It was obvious that Howard took his responsibility as a voter very seriously.

It wasn't until after the election that I finally learned how Howard had voted. Unfortunately, his vote had gone to the losing candidate, but that vote must certainly have been one of the best-researched, most carefully-thought-out votes that candidate received.

Howard's vote was just one out of millions. His candidate didn't even win. But Howard invested time and effort in making that voting decision as though it were the most important thing in the world. He felt a sense of responsibility to make the best possible choice, based on the best information he could obtain. He believed that vote was important.

Contrast Howard with Roger, who says every four years, "I just don't have time to go to the polls today. If I vote in the morning, I'll be late for work, and at the end of the day, I'm just too tired to make that extra stop. Besides, my one little vote isn't going to make a bit of difference. It's just not worth the trouble, since it doesn't matter anyway." Roger freely admits he's never seen the inside of a voting booth.

Roger's attitude is a convenient one. It lets him avoid the inconvenience of voting. It saves him the time and effort it would take to analyze the campaign issues and select a candidate. It frees him from the responsibility that voting entails.

Roger saves himself a lot of trouble by convincing himself that his vote doesn't matter. By pretending that his vote isn't important to anyone else, he can justify the fact that voting isn't important to *him*.

Outside the voting booth is a pretty safe hiding place.

Just Li'l Old Me

This same line of reasoning can be used to hide from God. If we can convince ourselves that what we believe and say and do doesn't matter to God, then we can feel OK about not giving Him first place in our lives. After all, if He doesn't really care about me, then why should I worry about pleasing Him? It's a slightly twisted line of reasoning, but it can come in handy if we're looking for a hiding place. This particular logic makes it much easier for us to escape any responsibilities God has for us.

When we choose this hiding place, we generally do so because:

1. We fail to see God as a personal God.
2. We don't understand the concept of God's unconditional love.
3. We have no sense of our place or His purpose for us in a complex, confusing world.

Any or all of these conditions can make "outside the voting booth" an attractive hiding place. Let's look at the reasons.

You're On Your Own

Those of us who hide "outside the voting booth" tend to believe that calling on God for help should be reserved for times when we face life's major tragedies: the death of a loved one, a serious illness, a crippling accident, the loss of a job. We have a sense of God as an all-knowing, all-seeing caretaker of the universe—but we don't grasp that He is a *personal* God. We tell ourselves, consciously or unconsciously, that He is Someone to turn to when life has us beat, when we're absolutely at the end of our human resources, but He doesn't want to be involved in our day-to-day lives. We pay our respects to Him on Sundays and at weddings, funerals, and other occasions, but we figure we're on our own when we're faced with a tough decision, a strained relationship, or a sense of loneliness or frustration. After all, He has the whole world to run.

The Bible confirms only one aspect of this viewpoint; it confirms that God is the supreme, all-powerful sovereign who reigns over creation.

"How great is God—beyond our understanding! The

number of his years is past finding out" (Job 36:26).

"The heavens declare the glory of God; the skies proclaim the work of his hands" (Psalm 19:1).

"For this is what the Lord says—he who created the heavens, he is God; he who fashioned and made the earth, he founded it, . . .he says,'I am the Lord and there is no other' " (Isaiah 45:18).

God *is* a mighty God. We react with awe to the thought of his limitless power, His omniscience, His ability to call worlds into being with merely a word, and His timeless nature. He is greater, much greater, than anything we know; our minds can't ever fully understand Him.

The Bible clearly tells us, though, that in addition to being a sovereign God, He is also a personal God. In fact, some of the most powerful passages of Scripture are those that contrast God's infinite might with His infinitely loving care. Consider this passage:

"The Lord thundered from heaven;
the voice of the Most High resounded.
He shot his arrows and scattered the enemies,
great bolts of lightning and routed them.
The valleys of the sea were exposed
and the foundations of the earth laid bare
at your rebuke, O Lord,
at the blast of breath from your nostrils.
He reached down from on high and
took hold of me;
he drew me out of deep waters.
He rescued me from my powerful enemy,
from my foes, who were too strong for me.
They confronted me in the day of my disaster,
but the Lord was my support.
He brought me out into a spacious place;

he rescued me because he delighted in me."
(Psalm 18:13-19)

Jesus, of course, was the ultimate expression of God's personal concern and His willingness and desire to be involved intimately and fully in every aspect of our lives. When Jesus portrayed Himself as standing at the door of our hearts, knocking, awaiting our invitation, He vividly illustrated God's personal interest in us.

Jesus also used down-to earth statements to describe God's concern for each of us:

"Are not five sparrows sold for two pennies? Yet not one of them is forgotten by God. Indeed, the very hairs of your head are all numbered. Don't be afraid; you are worth more than many sparrows" (Luke 12: 6-7).

Okay, What's the Catch?

So much that we desire in life has to be earned: material possessions, career advancement, educational degrees, financial security, prestige on the job or in the community. Sometimes we even feel that love and friendship have to be earned.

Several years ago, a friend of mine called to invite my family to her house for dinner. During the preceding several months, as it happened, we had been to their house a number of times but they hadn't been to ours. "We'd love to come," I told her, "but why don't you come over here instead? I think it's our turn."

"I haven't been keeping score," my friend replied. "I just want to see you."

We went to her house.

That conversation made me realize how foolish I had been to think that, after all our years of friendship, it mattered what the "score" was: how many times each family had been in the other's home. Yet that tit-for-tat mentality creeps into so many aspects of our lives. If a co-worker pitches in to help when we're under the gun, we wonder if we'll be obligated to help the next time he or she is in a jam. When one spouse unexpectedly takes responsibility for a certain household task, the other might wonder what task he or she will need to do to "even the score." When we borrow a neighbor's ladder, we assume that we're obligated to let him borrow something in the future—although he may have no intention whatsoever of doing so.

For some reason, we seem to be scorekeepers by nature. Maybe that's why it's so hard for us to understand that God's love for us—His personal, fatherly love for us as individuals—is unconditional. He gives it without expecting anything in return; in fact, He gives it knowing we're not capable of returning it in kind. It's the essence of His grace.

Recently I heard a rabbi speak about Jewish traditions related to death and mourning. He said that within the Jewish faith it is considered very important to attend the funeral of a friend or relative, *because it is an act of kindness that can never be repaid.*

For me, attending funerals was a way to demonstrate love and respect for the deceased and support for those left behind. The rabbi's words showed me a whole new meaning in that practice.

When we hide from God behind a sense of our own unimportance, we do so because we feel we haven't done anything to earn His love and concern. We tell ourselves we're just ordinary folks, not preachers or missionaries or Bible scholars. We haven't done anything outstanding that would be of interest to God.

This line of thought converts neatly to a self-reinforcing

philosophy that enables us to escape commitment indefinitely:
- (a) I haven't done anything for God; therefore,
- (b) He isn't interested in me; therefore,
- (c) I don't have to do anything for Him because He isn't interested in me.

Insert the acceptance of God's unconditional love into that circle, and the philosophy no longer works. Once we accept that God loves us without keeping score, then everything changes. We are loved. We are important. What we do matters. The mighty God who reigns over the universe has a personal interest in us. We can respond to that love by living lives of commitment and service, not just because we owe Him—but because He has come to dwell within us.

I've Lost My Place

Some time ago I went to a huge awards dinner held at a large hotel in the city. Since someone from our organization was receiving an award, the company I worked for had reserved a whole table. I arrived a little late, only to find that the person who handled the reservations had miscalculated, and there was no seat left at the table for me. I ended up sitting through the entire meal and lengthy program, not with my friends and co-workers, but with a table full of strangers who happened to have an empty place. They were gracious and made an effort to be friendly, but I still felt awkward and out of place. My presence at their table was more or less an accident; I didn't belong there. I had no role or identity among them. Understandably, I was glad when the evening was over.

The world in which we live can produce this same feeling of being out of place, of being someplace where we have no purpose or identity. If we feel that we are simply here by some accident of nature, then we're likely to be plagued by a nagging uncertainty as to what exactly we are supposed to do with our lives and what we are to accomplish. Our lifetimes are so short and our capacities are so limited, surely what we do or don't do can't matter much in the vast scheme of things. We have no sense of our place, our role, in the world. We can easily identify with the psalmist who wrote, "I am a stranger on earth" (Psalm 119:19). We look at what goes on around us and feel bewildered. We try to make sense of international events and the puzzle pieces don't fit. The people and events around us often create confusion, anxiety, or even pain. Then, just when we have gotten used to the world operating in a certain way, some drastic change occurs which forces us to re-think our views.

The psalmist knew the secret to understanding our place in the world. After he said, "I am a stranger on earth," he asked God, "Do not hide your commands from me." God's Word is our guidebook to living in this world; His Spirit is our constant resource.

Only God can see how all the pieces of the puzzle fit together; only He knows what unique role He has designed each of us to play. He ordered the universe, and its secrets are known only to Him. As long as we hide from Him, avoiding His commands, we will never have a sense of belonging, a sense of our purpose here.

I'm Okay, But I'm Not So Sure About You

When we hide from God under the cover of our own insignificance, we also lose sight of the importance of other people. We blind ourselves to their distinct and precious identities as children of God or potential brothers and sisters in Christ and fail to appreciate their unique gifts and qualities. We look at them only with human eyes, not with the loving eyes of our Creator.

As a result, we grow jealous when others threaten to outshine us—when they dress better, receive more praise for their work, make more money, or play a better game of tennis. We discount their successes and achievements so that we'll feel better about our own; we complain about their personality quirks and become impatient with their mistakes. We magnify their shortcomings so that our own are less glaring. In short, instead of actively seeking what is best in others, we pounce on their weaknesses and failings.

When we feel unimportant ourselves, we do things to help us view others as unimportant, too. Let's drop in on a business function to see this process at work:

At their company's annual Christmas party, Roy and Charlie are talking with a sales representative, Bert, from a manufacturing company that does business with their firm. In the course of the the conversation, Bert mentions that his hobby is mountain climbing, and he tells Roy and Charlie about some of the funny and exciting experiences he's had.

Later that evening, at home, Roy's wife asks him how the Christmas party was. "Great!" he tells her. "I talked to this guy from XYZ Manufacturing. He's had the most incredible experiences in mountain climbing. It was really interesting to hear about some of the things he's done. There's a guy with nerves of steel!"

The next morning, Charlie runs into Roy in the hall. Charlie says, "Boy, could you believe that big mouth from XYZ? What a show-off, trying to impress us with his mountain climbing stories. Bragging about his escapades like he thinks he's some super-hero or something. Who cares about all that? He probably made it all up anyway."

Charlie and Roy certainly have different viewpoints,

don't they? It's hard to believe they were talking about the same person. Roy, open to meeting someone new and learning about a hobby he didn't know much about, was excited and entertained by hearing about Bert's experiences. Charlie, on the other hand, afraid that someone else would come across as more interesting or more accomplished that he, felt the need to discredit Bert's stories. Insecure about his own importance, he wants to make Bert seem unimportant, too.

I see this kind of behavior all the time, not just in the business world but in social settings, too. We miss so much of the richness of human diversity when we leap at the chance to tear other people down.

When we hide from God's loving care and sink in our own sense of unimportance, we view the world from the perspective that we are all-important and that everything hinges on our wants and needs. We're so focused on ourselves, and so busy protecting our egos, that we miss out on the richness and the joy of discovering what other people are about. Charlie was so busy being afraid Bert would outshine him that he couldn't just sit back and enjoy Bert's adventures. I'd suspect that Charlie is the same guy who criticizes other people's ideas in business meetings, won't support any plan that he didn't come up with, and fights with the referees at the company basketball games.

Even though he is a Christian, Charlie doesn't have the fundamental sense of the value God sees in him, so he has to constantly boost his own ego at the expense of others. How much more he would enjoy life if he could open himself to the wealth of positive relationships and enjoyment of the differences in God's most complex and beloved creations.

The book of Proverbs tells us that, "He who seeks good finds good will" (11:27). When we focus on what is fascinating and unique and challenging in others, our eyes are opened to treasures that enrich our lives a hundredfold. The resulting relationships add a dimension to our lives that cannot be gained in any other way.

It's My Turn

Our place in the world is given to us by God's grace, through Christ. It's a part of the blessing that comes with knowing Him.

When we think about it, isn't it exciting to realize that not only has God given us a place of value in this world—as well as in eternity—but also that the role He has for us to fulfill here is custom-designed just for us? Doesn't it give you a sense of expectation, an eagerness to see what He has in store for you in your walk with Him?

The writers of Psalms often expressed that same sense of expectation. "In the morning, O Lord, you hear my voice; in the morning I lay my requests before you and wait in expectation" (Psalm 5:3).

"Come and see what God has done, how awesome his works in man's behalf!" (Psalm 66:5).

"Come and listen, all you who fear God; let me tell you what he has done for me" (66:16).

Our lives as children of God are meant to be ones of challenge and excitement. We only live this kind of life, though, when we come out of hiding, when we stop standing outside the voting booth, and instead, participate actively in our own spiritual growth. The excitement begins when we stop hiding from God behind a cover of false humility and say, "Yes, I am important to God and I have an important job to do for Him."

We can cultivate a greater awareness of our belonging, our role as members of God's family on earth. Outlined below are a few of the ways we might carry out these "spiritual exercises" in our daily life.

1. Practice giving and receiving unconditionally.

Grace is God's unconditional acceptance of us. He doesn't keep score; He knows we can't repay His goodness. We can understand His grace better when we practice both giving and receiving without the expectation of staying "even."

Let's break away from the scorekeeping mentality so prevalent around us. Let's challenge ourselves to do an act of kindness that cannot be repaid. Let's look around for a need we can meet—perhaps anonymously.

If someone goes out of his way for you or gives you a gift, accept it with grace and thanks. Don't let your mental calculator start tallying what you need to do to "even things up." Monitor your own thinking; be alert for trains of thought that lead to scorekeeping or "conditional" giving.

Two women I know, Cathy and Lona, have a longstanding friendship that epitomizes the concept of unconditional giving and receiving. Recently, when Cathy had to go out of town on a business trip, she was concerned about missing a whole week's worth of the night classes she was taking at a local university. Without even being asked, Lona volunteered to go to the classes and tape the instructor's lectures. If Cathy had to keep score, she would find it a cumbersome task to repay all those hours Lona spent sitting in classes on her behalf. As it was, she just accepted Lona's gracious gesture unconditionally—the way Lona had given it.

2. Cultivate a sense of our place in the world.

One of the boldest steps we can take toward coming out of hiding is to see clearly the incredibly complex and special creatures God has created as individual human beings. Look around you at the people you encounter every day. Each one is different. Each has his or her unique strengths and weaknesses, unique talents, unique combination of experiences and the lessons learned from them. When I was teaching college journalism, it didn't take me long to see that if I assigned 20 students to write virtually the same news story, when the assignment was completed I would have 20 different versions!

What special assets has God given you to contribute to the body of Christ? What tasks has He uniquely equipped you to do?

Take an inventory of your gifts and special strengths. In Romans 12:6-8 Paul lists certain gifts God gives to the members of the body of Christ. This list includes (but is not limited to!):

prophecy
service
teaching
encouragement
contributing to the needs of others
leadership
showing mercy

"Above all, love each other deeply, because love covers a multitude of sins. Offer hospitality to one another without grumbling. Each one should use whatever gift he has received to serve others, faithfully administering God's grace in its various forms," God told us in I Peter 4: 8-10.

Which of these gifts do you see in yourself? God commands us to know His gifts to us—to think of ourselves with "sober judgment, in accordance with the measure of faith God has given you" (Romans 12:3).

In I Corinthians 12:4-6 Paul says, "There are different kinds of gifts, but the same Spirit. There are different kinds of service but the same Lord. There are different kinds of working, but the same God works all of them in all men."

Fully exploring the nature of God's gifts is an entire study in itself, but being aware of them helps us take inventory of the gifts God has given us to use for Him. Exploring, cultivating, and cherishing our gifts from God not only helps us mature spiritually, but reaffirms our sense of having a place that is ours alone in His plan.

3. *Seek God's direction for fulfilling the role he has for us.*

My husband I don't go out for the evening very often. Our lives are hectic, and we like to spend our free time with our son rather than at social engagements. Sometimes, though, we do find ourselves preparing to attend some evening function that entails lining up a babysitter, dressing up, leaving instructions as to where we can be reached, and heading for our destination. Because we live in a large metropolitan area, obtaining directions to the location of the event is often another essential step in preparing to go.

More than once, after all the rushing around to get ready, we've found ourselves sitting in our car in our own driveway, looking at each other blankly as we realize we've forgotten to bring the directions. It's frustrating—and extremely humbling!

Taking inventory of our gifts from God without a sense of how He would have us use them leaves us in a similar predicament. An important step in coming out of hiding and into a sense of our place in God's world is seeking His guidance in how He would have us serve Him. Prayer, study of the Bible, the counsel and example of faithful Christians, openness and sensitivity to the Spirit's leading—all these things help us determine God's direction for us. Our lives are not static, and the Christian life is one of constant growth, change, and challenge. Where we are today is different from where we were yesterday and where we will be tomorrow. What a thrilling journey when we follow God's leading from place to place!

"You have made known to me the path of life; you will fill me with joy in your presence, with eternal pleasures at your right hand" (Psalm 16:11).

— 7 —

Hiding Place # 6: Among the Crowd

The Unknown Cowboy Makes An Appearance

Several years ago, my sister and I managed to coordinate our families' vacations so that all of us, along with our mother, could spend the week together at a dude ranch in the West. One of the long-standing traditions at the ranch was for the guests to put on entertainment for the staff on Saturday nights. The staff sang songs and performed skits for the guests on other nights during the week, but on Saturday, the tables were turned.

Our family group decided to sing a revised version of a popular folk song, rewritten as a ballad describing things that had occurred during the week. We worked industriously, practiced diligently, and anticipated the arrival of Saturday with enthusiasm.

All of us, that is, except my 13-year-old nephew, John. He was absolutely horrified at the thought of having to stand up in front of everyone—including the other teenagers he had been "hanging out" with all week—with his family ("This is so gross!") to sing a corny, homespun song. It was almost more than his tender teenage sensibilities could handle.

My sister, however, was adamant in her insistence that

since John was a part of the family, he was also to be part of the performance.

And he was. However, when it was our turn to go to the front of the room and sing, John disappeared into the hallway, and returned immediately with a paper sack over his head. His eyes were barely visible through the cut-out holes. He took his place with the rest of us and sang dutifully, while we tried not to break up into laughter before the song was finished.

Needless to say, the audience loved his caper, and it has gone down it our family's history as the "Visit of the Unknown Cowboy."

For my nephew, the bottom line regarding the family's "performance" was that he didn't want to be embarrassed by participating in what he viewed as an intolerably hokey activity, out of keeping with his "cool" image. Although he took a humorous approach to solving his problem, his desire to avoid looking foolish in front of his friends was very real. Being accepted by their peers is, as we know, a top priority for teenagers. They don't want to do anything that would make them stand out or seem like an oddball.

Teenagers, though, certainly aren't the only ones who feel that way. All of us like to hide among the crowd to some extent. We don't like to look different, be different, or act different from others who make up our peer group. We don't want to feel like the one member of the 200-piece marching band who heads toward the wrong end of the football field during the halftime show. Or the driver who heads the wrong way down a one-way street.

Even the Apostle Peter, who loved and served Jesus with such fervor during his earthly ministry, tried to hide among the crowd after Jesus was arrested. When someone recognized him as one of Jesus' followers, he denied even knowing Jesus. Think of how his heart must have lurched when he heard the cock crow and realized that Jesus' prophecy about his denial had come true (John 13: 31-38).

What makes us want to hide like this? Why do we want to lose ourselves among a sea of anonymous faces and nameless individuals rather than standing on our own, being willingly and noticeably different from others?

I believe we cower in this particular hiding place because we want to avoid exposing ourselves to criticism or ridicule. We don't want to risk being embarrassed by viewpoints or behavior other people will think is strange. Doing or saying things that set us apart from others erodes our sense of belonging, our unofficial membership in whatever group or groups are important to us. In addition, we don't want to give people anything to talk about behind our backs—although generally they will, no matter what we do!

"Sticks and stones may break my bones. . ."

In spite of our childhood rhyme that "words can never hurt me," we still are afraid of words. We fear what other people might say.

Amy is a talented advertising professional. She has an offbeat way of looking at the world that often results in amazingly fresh and creative approaches to selling her clients' products. When her co-workers are struggling to find new ideas, and are stuck in ruts because "that's the way we've always done it," she's the first to say "Why?" or "Can't we try it this way?"

Yet in her department's weekly meetings, when the group is brainstorming new ideas for advertising and promotional campaigns, Amy is nearly silent. One day a friend asked her why, when she had so many good ideas, she didn't speak up in the meetings.

Amy said it's because she's afraid of what the others in the meeting might say about her ideas.

"I guess that deep down I'm just afraid that I'll bring up an idea and someone will say, 'Boy, that's a dumb idea,' or 'That would never work.' Maybe someone would even laugh at my suggestion. I'd just die. I'd feel so embarrassed."

Think for a moment about the power of words. The one word "Fire!" can clear a crowded restaurant in minutes. The words "I love you" can change the course of a relationship forever. The statement "You can't be cured" puts life into an entirely new perspective.

Amy was afraid of words. She just couldn't face the prospect of hearing "That's a silly idea," so she simply never ventured an opinion in the meetings.

Last spring my husband coached our son's Little League team. When the season neared its end and the time came for the leagues' all-star team to be announced, my son was among the players selected. But his joy and excitement were short-lived. After his name was announced, one of his teammates told him, "You only made the all-star team because your dad's one of the coaches."

This spring, he decided to try out for his school's baseball team instead of Little League. When he learned that he had made the team, he said, "At least now no one can say I made the team because my dad was the coach." The pain caused by his teammate's words, spoken months earlier, was still there.

Words can hurt so much. Things other people say can affect our whole image of ourselves, erode our self-confidence, humiliate us, strike at our very hearts, destroying fragile self-images and even the will to live.

No wonder we're afraid of words.

The Bible tells us that words are powerful. Yet our fear

of words often faces in the wrong direction. We are deathly afraid of the words of others—yet maybe we aren't afraid enough of our own words.

The biblical writer James says the tongue is "a restless evil, full of deadly poison...Out of the same mouth come praise and cursing" (James 3:8-10).

"A gentle answer turns away wrath, but a harsh word stirs up anger. The tongue of the wise commands knowledge, but the mouth of the fool gushes folly" (Proverbs 15:1-2).

"Do not go about spreading slander among your people," God commanded the Israelites (Leviticus 19:16).

Jesus, too, warned us to pay careful attention to our words.

"But I tell you that men will have to give account on the day of judgment for every careless word they have spoken. For by your words you will be acquitted, and by your words you will be condemned" (Matthew 12:36-37).

Whew! Now we know why our mothers always told us, "Think before you speak." Even my father, who was not given to quoting the Bible, impressed upon me from my youngest days the psalmist's prayer: "May the words of my mouth and the meditation of my heart be pleasing in your sight, O Lord..." (Psalm 19:14).

A healthy fear of the power of our own words can prompt us to speak with greater caution and discretion. A constant awareness of our accountability before God can help us stifle that tempting bit of gossip before it slips out, nip that unkind retort, reconsider the truth of what we're about to say, and temper our criticism of those around us. As a result, we'll find ourselves less often facing the uncomfortable I-wish-I-hadn't-said-that feeling that arises when our words get out of control.

At the same time, as we become more vigilant about our

own words, we grow less concerned about what others say and less consumed by our fear of their words. If Amy focuses on being sure her own words are kind, gracious, and well-thought-out, she can spend less time and energy worrying about what someone else might say about her ideas. If she concentrates on being positive in the meeting, contributing to the group effort, and being encouraging and supportive to others, she'll help set a tone in which her ideas can be received with courtesy even if they're not adopted. And if people say, "That's crazy; it would never work," or even, "Boy, there's a real loser of an idea!" then they, not she, are the ones who have shown themselves to be lacking in diplomacy.

The reality of everyday life is that human beings do say things that hurt one another. We make insensitive remarks without considering how they will affect someone else. We try to shore up our own weak self-images by belittling others. We pass along juicy tidbits of gossip without weighing the effect they might have on the person we're talking about about—and this isn't something only women do, gentlemen!

Ouch! That hurts!

By relying on the Holy Spirit to help us control our tongues, we can keep from being on the "giving" end of hurtful words, but it's inevitable that we'll be on the receiving end from time to time. Hiding "among the crowd"—trying not to do anything that will cause us to be criticized or ridiculed—doesn't make any difference. Sometime, somewhere, someone will say something that hurts us.

If hiding isn't the answer, what can we do? How can we protect ourselves from the pain others' words can cause? We can't. But when we're on the receiving end of thoughtless or cruel or unkind words, we can deal with them from a biblical perspective and with a godly attitude.

The Bible tells us that the use of words to hurt others is simply a reflection of the sin nature (James 3:6). Human beings are subject to an ugly catalog of attitudes and behavior, and using words destructively is among them. Jesus said "What comes out of a man is what makes him 'unclean' " (Mark 7:20). Then, in verse 22 Jesus lists "slander"—often translated elsewhere as "gossip"—among the "evils that come from inside and make a man 'unclean.'"

Proverbs 6:16-19 lists seven things that are "detestable" to the Lord, and three of them have to do with what we say: "a lying tongue," "a false witness who pours out lies," and "a man who stirs up dissension among brothers."

Our words reflect what's in our hearts, and the hearts of men and women are not always filled with the mercy, love, and understanding that reflect who we are as children of God. The result? Unkind words. Malicious gossip. Lies about other people. Insults. Brutal criticism. Angry barbs. Manipulation and deceit.

The presence of these verbal bullets in our everyday world is as much a reality as the other evils of human life: murder, theft, corporate espionage, back-stabbing, cheating, adultery. They all stem from the dark qualities of a fallen human nature, and they will be with us until the day we see Christ. We cannot expect to hide successfully from others' hurtful words. Even if we never take risks or stand up for what we believe, never present a new idea or try a different way of doing something, every now and then a "bullet" is bound to hit us. Even if we try to keep a low profile about being a Christian, and try hard to fit in and look and act like everyone else, we can't avoid criticism forever. That's life in a real world dominated by Satan's active work (Ephesians 2:1-2).

If we let it, our fear of hurtful words will cripple both our spiritual walk and the pursuit of our life's goals. It will be a constant barrier standing between us and the rich, full life God wants for us. If, like Amy, we're unwilling to take risks because of what might be said about us, our talents will go unused and unnoticed, our dreams unrealized, our spiritual potential untapped.

Another important biblical principle is that the way we respond to others' words is a testimony to the Holy Spirit within us. The world cannot see the love of Christ and the grace of God inside our hearts; it only sees our actions that reflect their presence. How we respond to unkind or deceitful or malicious words is one way we demonstrate the qualities of the Holy Spirit. The Bible gives us numerous guidelines to show us how we are to respond:

"When we are cursed, we bless; when we are persecuted, we endure it; when we are slandered, we answer kindly," (I Corinthians 4:12-13).

". . .Set an example for the believers in speech, in life, in love, in faith and in purity" (I Timothy 4:12).

"Let your conversation be always full of grace, seasoned with salt, so that you many know how to answer everyone" (Colossians 4:6).

Rather than fearing that others will hurt us with their words, the Bible challenges us to be courageous, seizing those occasions as opportunities to demonstrate a Christ-like response.

For example:

Your co-worker Gene tells you, "I heard Joe in the break room telling everyone how you mixed up the data in that last monthly report. He said he had to re-do everything at the last minute. He made it sound like you really screwed up."

You could say, "That Joe is such a bigmouth. Yes, I pulled the wrong data, but it's not like he's never made a mistake. Maybe I should go into the break room and tell everybody how he was bragging about doing his quarterly summary at the last minute, and using his own estimates instead of actual figures because he didn't have time to pull them. Or maybe people would like to hear about his little trip out of town with the accounting manager that his wife doesn't know about."

Or, you could say, "Well, I was just glad Joe caught my mistake before the report was turned in. I wish he wouldn't tell everyone about it, but it's really no big secret. I sure don't plan to let it happen again!"

The Bible makes it clear that being criticized for our outlook, lifestyle, and other facets of the Christian life is inevitable. After all, the Bible tells us we are called to be misfits.

Wait a minute! "Called to be misfits?"

Yes! We are to be the band members out-of-step, the drivers going the "wrong" way—going God's direction on the world's one-way street to despair and emptiness. "If the world hates you, keep in mind that it hated me first. If you belonged to the world, it would love you as its own. As it is, you do not belong to the world, but I have chosen you out of the world" (John 15:18-19).

Or, as the Apostle Peter said, "Dear friends, I urge you, as aliens and strangers in the world, to abstain from sinful desires, which war against the soul. Live such good lives among the pagans that, though they accuse you of doing wrong, they may see your good deeds and glorify God on the day he visits us" (I Peter 2:11-12).

A local public relations executive startled the business

community a few years ago by making a major change in his life. He sold his shares in the large national public relations firm he managed and moved to the west coast to attend seminary. After struggling for many years to discern God's call in his life, he finally took the plunge.

Imagine the reactions he must have gotten when he announced his plans. People shook their heads and muttered things like "off the deep end". . ."midlife crisis". . ."crazy" when his name came up. How many people do you suppose said, "That's great!" or "I admire your decision"? How many people do you think really understood when he gave up his six-figure salary, prestigious position, pension plan, and other benefits so that he could "become a preacher"?

For him, God's call was the only truth that mattered. Some people saw that and some didn't, but other people's opinions weren't the basis for his decision.

Contrary to Popular Opinion. . .

For most of us, though, public opinion—that is, the opinion of those who matter to us—does influence our decisions a great deal more than we would like to admit. Why is it that, when we know the myriad weaknesses of human beings and how often their thoughts are contrary to God's, we still care so much what they think and say about us?

My son knew he had played well enough during the season to make the all-star team, but his friend's words shattered his confidence. He began to doubt himself. He put more faith in their opinion of him than his own experience.

It is part of our human nature to care about what people think of us. It's all part of that fundamental human desire to belong, to be accepted, to be included "in the crowd."

Jesus understands. After all, He was human, too, and more than anyone else, He knows that obeying God's call to be different isn't always easy.

He also knew that after His death His followers would have a hard time standing for Him without His physical presence to encourage them. Shortly before he was crucified, He prayed a loving and fervent prayer that they—and we—would be able to withstand the rigors of this out-of-step lifestyle, to cope with the pressures the world would constantly bring against them: "I have given them your word and the world has hated them, for they are not of the world anymore than I am of the world....Sanctify them by the truth; your word is truth. As you sent me into the world, I have sent them into the world" (John 17:14-17).

I'm Losing in the Popularity Polls

Recently I was moaning to a friend about the trials of being a writer in general, and a writer of Christian books in particular. I reenacted for him the conversation that so often occurs—at parties, for example—when I meet someone new and they learn that I write books.

New acquaintance: "How interesting! What kind of books do you write?"

Me: "Christian books—that is, books having to do with biblical issues."

New Acquaintance (subtly moving away): "Oh."

Such a little word: "oh." And yet it conveys so much.

I haven't been able to decide whether people are simply not interested in hearing about books with a spiritual message, or if they feel threatened by the word "Christian" and want to make their escape before I can buttonhole them and say, "Are you saved?"

These conversations always leave me feeling embarrassed and deflated. I love writing books, and above all I love the new spiritual insights I gain in the process. It hurts when people react which such avoidance.

One of my friends, who is also a writer and a Christian, listened sympathetically, and then he said, "I think every time that happens, you're taking another stand for Christ, and I believe God will honor you for that. Being ignored or avoided like that is a form of persecution. The Bible tells us we'll be persecuted for our faith. Just because nobody is trying to stone you or openly ridiculing you doesn't mean you're not being persecuted."

Christians are not supposed to do things the world's way, because although we are in the world, we are not of the world. When we fail to follow the world's rules and standards, the world laughs at us, points at us, criticizes us, avoids us, gossips about us, and in general, fails to understand us.

Paul said we shouldn't be surprised. "The man without the Spirit does not accept the things that come from the Spirit of God, for they are foolishness to him, and he cannot understand them, because they are spiritually discerned" (I Corinthians 2:14).

Jesus, in fact, told us to rejoice in persecution: "Blessed are you when people insult you, persecute you and falsely say all kinds of evil against you because of me. Rejoice and be glad, because great is your reward in heaven. . ." (Matthew 5:11).

Although I worked at a Christian publishing company at one point in my career, most of the time during the past two decades I have worked for secular organizations. I've sat at lunch and heard a local church congregation—of which I was a member—categorically described as "weird." I've heard people on coffee breaks say, "Those 'born-again

Christians' drive me nuts." I've heard a co-worker become the object of jokes because of her active involvement in her church and seen another laughed at because she mentioned the teaching of Christ in a staff meeting. And that doesn't count the things that may have been said about me over the years that I haven't heard.

Even though the Bible warns us about it, it still hurts to be ridiculed. It hurts to feel that the "in" group considers you a part of the "out" group.

So, we look for ways to avoid that hurt. We work harder to fit in. We tell ourselves, "Well, maybe I won't say grace at lunch when I'm out with the other women from work," or "I won't tell Bill I can't go to the party because I have Bible study. I'll tell him it's because Joan and I made some plans to go out with friends."

It's so very, very tempting.

The Apostle Peter, of course, learned an agonizing lesson about denying Christ. Peter cared about other people's opinions. He was afraid to be identified with the Man from Galilee. Jesus had been arrested. The cause to which Peter had so completely devoted himself seemed lost. Inside Caiaphas's house, people were mocking Jesus, attacking Him for outlandish claims like being able to prophesy and to "destroy the temple of God and rebuild it in three days" (Matthew 26:61). Maybe, out there in the courtyard, Peter could even hear the angry accusations.

Peter was exhausted, physically and emotionally. How could he convince the people in Pilate's courtyard that yes, this man who had been arrested really was the Messiah, and yes, He would triumph over death. How could he make them understand the power of Jesus, the passion His words inspired, His miracles, His overwhelming love? No, Peter didn't want to risk their jokes or their anger. He had told Jesus earlier, "Even if I have to die with you, I will never disown you" (Matthew 26:35). But now, he just wanted to lose himself in the crowd. Like we sometimes do.

The Gospel writer Luke, in describing Peter's denial of Jesus, says that just as the cock crowed, "The Lord turned and looked straight at Peter" (Luke 22:61). What emotions do you suppose were on Jesus' face or in His eyes in that look? I believe there must have been many: Sorrow, disappointment, understanding, compassion, love—and forgiveness.

It would have been out of keeping with Jesus' character or divine nature for Him to turn against Peter for showing human weakness. Jesus had known it would happen; He knew Peter—just as He knows us—better than anyone. He knew Peter loved Him, but He also knew Peter was just a man. He knew Peter's spiritual strength was imperfect, and that the world's pressure would conquer him that day.

The Bible tells us that Peter "wept bitterly" (Matthew 26:75) when he heard the cock crow. Imagine how overcome with pain and self-loathing he must have been. Yet, he did not give up—not on Jesus, and not on himself. In fact, it's likely that the experience strengthened him, deepened his commitment, made him more aware of his own weaknesses so that he could rely more on God's strength.

Nor did Jesus give up on him. Peter was among those to whom Jesus appeared after His resurrection. Boldly empowered by the Holy Spirit, Peter became the church's greatest leader in the days after Jesus' death. He preached courageously in the face of opposition from the religious authorities and stood up for Christ even when it meant persecution and imprisonment. The man who denied

Jesus three times went down in history as the first great leader of the early church.

There is certainly a message of hope for us in Peter's story. We deny Jesus in little ways every day. We pass up opportunities to tell others the Good News of salvation. We fail to take a stand when the off-color jokes or the malicious rumors start. We make decisions based on what other people will think instead of on what He commands.

Jesus knows we do these things. Yet, just as He knew Peter's heart, He knows ours. He knows we love Him. He knows we want to live courageously for Him. He waits patiently for us to grow to maturity, and each time we falter, He strengthens us to go forward. Like Peter, we can put our past denials and failures behind us and go on to do great things for Him confident that when, on occasion, we give in to our human desire to stay hidden among the crowd, He forgives us.

"If we died with him,
we will also live with him;
if we endure,
we will also reign with him.
If we disown him,
he will also disown us;
if we are faithless,
he will remain faithful. . . ."
(II Timothy 2:11-13)

The prophet Micah says that what God requires of us is "to act justly and to love mercy and to walk humbly with your God" (Micah 6:8). Jesus emphasized that in Matthew 22:37-39. He told us the greatest of His commandments is to, "Love the Lord your God with all your heart and with all your soul and with all your mind. . . . And the second is like it: 'Love your neighbor as yourself.' To love

God, to love others, and to obey God's commandments. That's where the ultimate life of excitement and adventure lies. We may be laughed at, criticized, or gossiped about along the way, but what are a few unkind words compared to the fulfillment and joy of becoming a little more like Christ?

Overall, being a misfit feels pretty good.

—8—

Hiding Place # 7: Under the Bulldozer

Like many men and women of his generation, Michael served in the armed forces during the war in Southeast Asia. In 1968 he was stationed with the U.S. Marines at a base near DaNang, South Vietnam. His job was to service and repair trucks, bulldozers, and other heavy equipment.

Michael vividly remembers the first time the base was hit by enemy fire:

"I was working on this bulldozer and suddenly someone yelled 'Incoming!' I heard a mortar shell explode a little distance away. I grabbed my weapon and my helmet and without even thinking about it, I dove under the bulldozer. It was the only thing nearby that offered even the remotest cover from the shelling.

"I could see and hear the explosions and feel the ground shake. Everyone had taken cover. Some of the other engineers had slid under the other big vehicles. I knew if I came out from under that bulldozer, I'd probably be killed. I remember being so scared.... I'll never forget that feeling, not as long as I live. I was 20-years-old and, suddenly, that bulldozer was all that stood between me and being blown apart."

Life can be scary.

Because of the work I do, I travel a great deal. I often find myself in strange cities—Washington, D.C., Chicago, Atlanta—walking down hotel corridors alone, riding alone in cabs to my appointments, eating alone in restaurants. I think about the statistics on muggings and assaults, and sometimes I feel afraid. I have a black belt in karate and have studied self-defense for five years; I still feel afraid, and I don't like it.

When the enemy fire began, Michael was afraid for his life. When I am alone in a strange city, I am afraid for my physical safety.

But not all frightening situations stem from fear of physical danger. We fear the words and opinions of others; we don't like to make ourselves vulnerable to hurt. We fear the loss of things precious to us. We fear the future; we fear the unknown; we even fear uncertainty. And we fear failure—failure to accomplish what we said we would do; failure to meet our own or someone else's expectations; failure to measure up to an external or internal standard.

We cannot, however, live lives of challenge and adventure if we live in fear. Fear immobilizes us. It saps our strength. It keeps us from growing, from moving forward, and from taking risks. As a result, it keeps us from experiencing the fullness and excitement that is part of God's plan for us. We cannot make headway along the journey of faith if we stay under the bulldozer all the time.

I'm not talking about commonsense fear. In listening to Michael describe his experience under enemy fire, I doubt that anyone would say that he should have jumped out from under the bulldozer and yelled, "See, I'm not scared!" Nor would it be wise of me to walk city streets alone, late at night, to prove I'm not afraid. Common sense dictates that we respond to certain fears in sensible, practical ways. Yet, we need to confront other fears head-on, with boldness and faith, if we are to become what God wants us to be.

What are the bulldozers in your life, my life? What are the hiding places where we run for protection from the "dangers" of daring, front-line, courageous living?

1. The Plan

I love to watch reruns of the old TV adventure series, "The A-Team." The show is about a team of fearless, Robin Hood-type commandos who travel around the world extricating good guys from trouble by outsmarting bad guys. In the process, of course, the A-Team regularly ends up being pursued by federal authorities, the Highway Patrol, the local sheriff, and an ugly assortment of thugs, hoodlums, and international drug lords. The team is alternately thrown in jail, incarcerated in military prisons, slapped in Central American guerilla stockades, and "put on ice" in abandoned warehouses guarded by goons with automatic weapons. (Although each episode invariable includes car chases, shootouts, explosions and other noisy escapades, no one ever gets killed. It's implausible, but I like it.)

The leader of the A-Team is a former Army colonel named John "Hannibal" Smith. Hannibal always has a plan. No matter how bleak the situation looks, the team can always rely on Hannibal.

"Hannibal, have you got a plan for getting us out of this?" one of the team members will ask plaintively as he looks around the prison-of-the-day.

"Of course. I always have a plan," Hannibal answers calmly.

"Well, what is it?" another asks.

"I'm still working on it."

Whether Hannibal really has a plan at any given time or not, the team relies on his confidence in often-non-existent plans to reassure themselves that everything is going to turn out all right.

We like to have a plan, too. We like to chart the course of our lives, to make sure we know what's around the corner and how we're going to get from here to there. Having a plan gives us a sense of control, which, in turn, makes us feel secure. It's our hedge against uncertainty. We fear the unknown, and planning helps us feel that the future is more "known," more controllable.

Information to help us formulate our plans bombards us. Through the mail, in magazines, on TV, in books, at work, and in our community, we can find people telling us how to plan for just about everything: Insurance plans. Investment plans. Career plans. Wardrobe plans. Beauty plans. College plans. Vacation plans. Retirement plans. Funeral plans. Even spiritual growth plans.

How much planning does one person's life need? Naturally, it varies. Some personality types are more inclined to rely on planning than others. For instance, one extreme is Richard, the person who carefully formulates plans for each day, each week, and each year. His career is mapped out for the next twenty years, with specific three-and-five-year goals. His vacation plans are based on covering 392 miles per day at an average driving speed of 57.3 miles per hour, allowing 45 minutes each for breakfast, lunch and dinner. He has made reservations at motels along the way, with guaranteed late check-in, of course.

At the other extreme is Dan, the "free spirit," who gets up in the morning having no idea what the day holds. He remembers he has an appointment scheduled for "around three o'clock" at someone's office "up in the northeast part of town." He likes the job he has, but if he runs across one that sounds more interesting, he'll make a change. His vacation plans consist of getting into the car and driving.

If a sign along the way advertises a historic site or a tourist attraction that catches his interest, he stops and takes a look. When he's driven enough for one day, he finds a roadside campground and sleeps in the car.

Many times we approach life from these extremes!

Plans should be a reflection of common sense and practicality. If I have a major project at work to complete by April 1, I'd better do some planning so March 31 doesn't roll around and find me with the project undone. If I want to have ten friends over for dinner Friday night, I need to plan what I'm going to feed them, or I'll find myself at the convenience store that night buying canned soup and corn chips (which I have done!).

Sometimes, though, I believe we use excessive planning as a bulldozer, a place to hide from God's call to trust Him fully. To be honest, I don't know where the line is between common sense and failure to trust God. If I buy health insurance, does that mean I don't trust God to meet my needs if I should become seriously ill? If I don't let my son ride his bicycle to school because there are no sidewalks and I think it's dangerous, am I failing to trust God to protect him?

Like so many things, making plans is only an obstacle to spiritual growth if we let it become one. Planning our careers or our finances or our children's education isn't a sin. Only *when our own plans become more important than God's plans* do we run a spiritual risk.

Does this mean we don't make any plans of our own? Of course not. It simply means that we make those plans with the overriding goal to fulfill God's desires for us, not our own. When we make our plans with His commandments, His standards, His priorities in mind, then we can be confident of His blessing and guidance, whether the plans fall into place as we expect or not.

Sandra had her life pretty well planned out. She and Paul were married for several years before they decided to start a family; then she quit her job so she could be at home with the children. She loved being a full-time wife and mother and planned to continue doing so until her last child was out of school. Then, she thought, she'd get her real estate license or, perhaps, take some computer classes and find a job in the computer field. Eventually, she and Paul would both retire and do all the traveling they'd always talked about—including, of course, visits to their children and grandchildren.

After she and Paul had been married about ten years, Sandra learned that he was having an affair with a woman at his office. He announced to Sandra one night that he was divorcing her so he could marry this woman. She tried to convince him to go to counseling, to consider the needs of their children, to remember his Christian commitment. But, he wasn't interested. He left, and Sandra saw her entire life-plan disintegrate in a flash.

Even though she didn't have much specialized education or experience, Sandra had to take a full-time job to support herself and the children. Further education, retirement, travel—all those plans were just a memory. All she could think about was getting through each day, trying to maintain a stable home life for her children, and trying to meet their needs.

In the past, Sandra's plans had given her a sense of security and confidence. She felt she could look ahead and see her life unfolding into the future, knowing what it would hold. Now she doesn't know what the next hour holds. She's trying to do some financial planning so the children can go to college, and also trying to work out a way she can take some night classes. But she knows now that plans don't always come to pass the way we think they will. She's learned that man-made plans should always carry the warning, "subject to change."

Sandra's life isn't turning out the way she planned, but there are still choices to be made. She can choose to live in resignation and despair, or she can choose to live in renewed trust and confidence, "waiting in expectation" (Psalm 5:3). That won't exempt her from the pain of loss, adjustment, and change—but it will give her a bedrock of assurance that her life is in hands more capable than her own.

When we look to our own plans for our sense of security, we are, indeed, like the man who built his house on sand. "The rain came down, the streams rose, and the winds blew and beat against that house, and it fell with a great crash" (Matthew 7:27). When we make our plans under the condition and with the assurance that God is sovereign, we can withstand the pouring rain, the rising streams and the beating winds—because our foundation is on the Rock of Ages.

2. The Lifetime Guarantee

Learning to trust God in all aspects of our lives is a lifelong challenge. It's hard. We want guarantees. We want insurance and reassurance. And we want to be in control.

The irony is that only when we rely fully on God do we have those guarantees. The more completely we relinquish control, the more fully secure we can be. His plan for us is perfect, and His plan is for our good. Only He sees the eternal "big picture." Only He completely and intimately knows us, our capabilities, our weaknesses, our potential. Only He offers us a true lifetime guarantee.

"Lord, you have assigned me my portion and my cup;
you have made my lot secure.
The boundary lines have fallen for me

in pleasant places;
surely I have a delightful inheritance."
(Psalm 16:5-6)

Kurt is a salesman for an insurance company. He doesn't feel that he's cut out to be a salesperson; he's not particularly interested in insurance, and he doesn't much like his job at all. A few years ago, when his second child was born, he felt his family needed more money to meet their additional expenses. The insurance sales job paid better than the one he had in the business office of a large hospital, so when it was offered to him, he felt he should accept it.

His wife, Rita, sees that his unhappiness in his job affects everything about their lives. He seems to have lost his zest for living. Although he's still a devoted husband and father, he feels so trapped in his job that he can't see beyond it. It's as though just getting through each day is a chore for him.

Deep down, what Kurt would really like to do is become a paramedic. He feels that he's cool in a crisis and good at making decisions under pressure. His work in the hospital gave him an understanding of the medical field, and, above all, he wants to have a job where he can truly help people in need.

The local junior college offers a two-year course. Kurt stopped by and picked up an application form, along with information about scholarships, but he hasn't filled it out. Even though Rita asks him about it every now and then, he always gives her some vague answer about being too busy or forgetting about it. She's told him several times that she's willing to go to work to support the family while he's in school.

Actually, Kurt has avoided filling out the application because he's plagued by doubts. *What if this isn't the right move for me*? he wonders. *What if I graduate and I can't get a job? What if, at 37, I'm just too old to be starting a new career?*

How would you advise Kurt if he came to you?

Perhaps you and I, as his friends, might help him analyze the situation by encouraging him to ask himself these questions:

a. Is this choice in harmony with my understanding of what God wants for me?

Kurt's interest in becoming a paramedic stems from a desire to use his talents and skills and to be of help to others. There certainly doesn't seem to be anything in his motivation that's contrary to God's will. If anything, pursuing this new career will give Kurt new opportunities to use the unique skills and experience God has given him.

b. Will anyone else suffer if I make this choice?

While Kurt may feel that the financial consequences of this change will have a negative impact on his family, Rita believes that the family will ultimately be better off if he is happy and satisfied in his work. She feels that the financial sacrifices they might need to make while he's in school will be well worth it and besides, she's confident that God will meet their needs. She likes the example Kurt will be setting for their children, demonstrating for them a willingness to trust God and to accept a new challenge even when the outcome isn't guaranteed.

c. In what ways will this choice enhance my walk with Christ?

Simply by trusting God to see him through this career change, Kurt will be growing spiritually. Later on, as he deals daily with life-and-death situations, he'll have more and more opportunities to depend on God's guidance and wisdom. In relation to his co-workers, his patients, their families and others, he'll have countless opportunities to demonstrate a Christ-like spirit.

d. What spiritual pitfalls will I need to watch out for in making this decision?

Often, when we make a choice and it proves to be a good one, and we are successful at what we have undertaken, we're tempted to take all the credit. If Kurt does especially well in his school work and lands a good job, he may be tempted to believe it's because he's a pretty talented guy, a courageous risk-taker, a fellow who knows how to take charge of his life. All that will probably be true—yet it will be true only because God has blessed Kurt and enabled him to achieve his goals. We exist, we succeed, we even survive only at God's pleasure. His blessing is cause for continual thanksgiving—not continual self-congratulation.

By the same token, if something goes awry in Kurt's progress toward his goal—perhaps he becomes ill and has to drop out of school, or Rita is laid off her job and he has to go back to work—he'll face the temptation to despair, or to become angry at God, or to abandon his dreams. As Sandra learned, things don't always go according to our plans, even when we are confident those plans have God's blessing.

"'For I know the plans I have for you,' declares the Lord, 'plans to prosper you and not to harm you, plans to give you hope and a future. Then you will call upon me...and I will listen to you. You will seek me and find me when you seek me with all your heart'" (Jeremiah 29:11-13).

Our job in difficult, stressful situations is to remain faithful in the face of disappointment and to remain confident that we are still in God's keeping. It isn't His plan that's gone awry, it's only ours. His is still intact, and if we continue to rely on Him and seek His will, His plan for our good will ultimately be realized. We may just need to make adjustments in our own.

"All the days ordained for me were written in your book before one of them came to be" (Psalm 139:16). That's our lifetime guarantee. It's the only one we need.

3. *The Fail-Safe System*

Human beings hate failure. We'll do all sorts of bizarre things to avoid it. We'll give up a dream rather than risk failing to reach it. We'll tell ourselves we're unlovable or incompetent or stupid, and thus talk ourselves out of trying something at which we may not succeed. We'll discount the success of others to avoid feeling like we've fallen short ourselves. We tell ourselves it's okay to hide under the protective bulldozer because no one wants to get hurt by failure.

When an opportunity to apply for a great new job comes along, we'll find any excuse not to apply: "I couldn't find a pen for filling out the application form." That way, we don't have to risk not being selected for the position.

When the local theater group holds tryouts for a play, we're just "too busy" to go—even though we've always dreamed of being on stage. That way we don't have to face the possibility of not getting the part we want.

John is a computer consultant. Like many people who are proficient with computers, he has a very logical, orderly mind that thinks in terms of cause and effect, practicality and rational reasoning. He was telling me one evening about a conversation he had with his teenage son about trying out for the school soccer team. He knew Johnny wanted to play soccer, but the week tryouts were to begin, Johnny said he wasn't trying out.

"Why?" his dad asked him.

"Because I might not make it," Johnny answered.

"And what will happen if you don't make it?" John asked.

Johnny thought for a minute, and then said, "I guess I won't be on the team."

"And what will happen if you don't try out at all?" was his dad's next question.

"I won't be on the team."

"So what do you have to lose by trying out?"

Pause.

"Nothing."

Johnny did try out for the team—and he didn't make it. He was disappointed. He saw, though, that he hadn't really lost anything. And he had gained an important lesson: that failing to succeed or obtain a goal doesn't mean the end of the world.

I think all of us could use a dose of John's practical advice from time to time. We get so caught up in the emotions of failure that we're unable to see it from a logical perspective, a perspective that prompts us to ask, "What do I really have to lose by trying?"

Fear of failure locks us into a life of limitations and barriers. It keeps us from expanding our horizons, exploring our God-given capabilities, seeking new relationships and cultivating spiritual courage. It keeps us from taking chances, from being willing to trust ourselves in the confidence that God has given us a unique potential—and expects us to use it for Him!

We worry about how other people's opinion of us will be affected if we try something and don't succeed. We fear what they'll say about us. As much as anything, we fear the negative feelings that accompany failure. Self-doubt. Embarrassment. A sense of defeat. The feeling that we were foolish to try, that we're not good enough or talented enough or smart enough to succeed at this or that.

Yet all these feelings represent a choice. Whether or not we attain what we set out to attain—a job promotion, a part in the play, a lasting relationship—may be largely outside our control. Those decisions often aren't completely up to us. What we can always choose, though, is whether or not to accept an attitude of failure. An attitude of failure is an attitude of fear and self-doubt. It's an attitude that says, "Don't try." It's an attitude that says God isn't as wise, as dependable, or as sovereign as He says He is. It's an attitude that says God didn't do a very good job when He made you or me.

I don't think an attitude of failure is a biblical one.

Even when we undertake something that we sincerely believe to be God's will for us, there's no guarantee we'll succeed. The "prosperity theology," or "success theology" we discussed in the the chapter on hiding "in the warehouse" dictates the belief that God wants us to turn everything we touch into gold, to be successful by the *world's* standards in everything we do. I just can't find anything in God's Word to support it, to make me believe that's part of His design for our spiritual walk.

First of all, this present world system and its standards are ruled by the prince of darkness (I Corinthians 2:4-10). Secondly, if we were to succeed by the world's definition at everything we try, why would the biblical writer James feel compelled to tell us to, "Consider it pure joy. . . whenever you face trials of many kinds, because you know that the testing of your faith develops perseverance. Perseverance must finish its work, so that you may be complete, not lacking anything" (James 1:2-4). Failing to get the things we want is part of our spiritual training, because it teaches us to persevere, to rely on God, to be faithful in the face of discouragement, to trust His judgment as to what is best for us.

However, neither do I believe in "failure theology," (a term I just coined) which proposes that if we try something and don't do well at it, we're failures, and that's just God's way of slapping us down and keeping us in line. The problem with "failure theology" is that it doesn't conform to the spiritual model God gave us when He sent Christ into the world.

We are imperfect, sinful. Christ died so that we would not have to pay the ultimate penalty for our sin, our "failure" to be perfect as Christ is perfect. His loving sacrifice alone stands between us and the death penalty for our sins. If Christ died to redeem our spiritual failures, and continually forgives us when we confess them, then why should we become locked in by our earthly failures, which are so much less important?

God has invested so much in us—in creating us in His image, in giving us a unique, personalized role in His church and His world. Our ups and downs of success and failure are simply part of the process of discovering more fully areas of growth He intends for us to know. If we avoid all experiences and situations that might hold the possibility of failure, then we cut ourselves off from that process, and we stifle the potential for spiritual maturity God intends for us. If, on the other hand, we view each attempt at something new—a new job, a new relationship, a new idea, a new skill, a new activity—as part of the discovery process, then we "win" regardless of the outcome, because we learn something about the God who made us.

"Have I not commanded you? Be strong and courageous. Do not be terrified; do not be discouraged, for the Lord your God will be with you wherever you go" (Joshua 1:9).

Win or lose. Succeed or fail. Look like a hero or look like a dunce. He's there. That's our fail-safe assurance.

4. The Ultimate Loss

I will never forget the night my father died. My mother and I had visited the hospital and then stopped for something to eat when we left. Just as we got home, the telephone rang. We both answered it at the same time, on different extensions. "Mr. Maynard has expired," the nurse at the other end said.

And that was that. The end of a life. Just like that. My father was lost to me forever.

No wonder we are afraid of death. It is so unfathomable, such a stark contrast to the constant activity and busyness of our lives. Its "forever-ness," its permanence, like God's infinity, are beyond our mental grasp. It is the outer boundary of what we understand.

Death is the ultimate loss, the loss of all that we know. And just as we fear it, we also fear other losses ranging from the loss of material things to the loss of our children's innocence, and everything in between. We fear the loss of prestige or power or reputation...the loss of youth and physical beauty...the loss of a marriage relationship or a child's love. We fight to protect ourselves against the loss of control, of love, of security. We hide from life's challenges and adventures because we know that at its end there is always death. We let it give us a sense of futility rather than a sense of freedom.

Human existence is so filled with irony. One of the great mysteries of the Christian life is that we begin to possess true riches only when we are willing to lose everything else. This theme occurs inescapably throughout the Bible. When we hide under the bulldozer because we are afraid of loss, we prevent ourselves from coming into the untold riches of our spiritual inheritance.

"Whoever finds his life will lose it, and whoever loses his life for my sake will find it" (Matthew 10:39). Christ's sacrifice on the cross liberates us from the fear of death. God's Word liberates us from the fear of loss.

The Apostle Paul didn't see death as a loss at all. "For to me," he wrote, "to live is Christ and to die is gain" (Philippians 1:21). In human terms, death is the ultimate loss; in spiritual terms, it is the ultimate reward, uniting us with God in the eternal life He promised. Similarly, our smaller losses in day-to-day life are a form of gain, too, as they free us from our enslavement to the world and help us focus our sights on heaven.

"The Lord is my light and my salvation—," the psalmist wrote, "whom shall I fear? The Lord is the stronghold of my life—of whom shall I be afraid?" (Psalm 27:1).

Doctors and psychologists who deal with terminally ill individuals have discovered that often the diagnosis of a fatal illness has the effect of liberating the patient. The person says in effect, "Well, I have about six months of life left. Now I can finally stop doing all these things I don't want to do and start living the way I want to." That person has been freed from the musts and shoulds of human life, the petty constraints imposed by society or personal ambitions. He is free from the fear of loss; his entire life appears in a new light. He no longer needs to fear being hurt by other's words or actions. Material wealth and possessions no longer mean anything because he knows they will soon end anyway. By seeing his life nearing its end, he recognizes the temporary nature of the things around him.

If we can learn to recognize this "temporariness" before a doctor's grim prognosis, we can become free from the fear of losses of all kinds. When we acknowledge that life itself is temporary, we feel a new sense of urgency to pick up the pace of our day-to-day discovery of God's plan for us. We have a renewed desire to undertake a "cram course" in spiritual growth and adventurous living as we prepare for eternity.

When we acknowledge that relationships are temporary, we work harder to make the most of them, yet we are also better able to accept it if they don't work out.

When we acknowledge that material wealth and possessions are temporary, we can invest less of our time and effort in accumulating and maintaining them, and more to meeting the needs of those less fortunate.

What a refreshing lifestyle we could have if we could learn to be truly free of the fear of loss!

> "As for man, his days are like grass,
> he flourishes like a flower of the field;
> the wind blows over it and it is gone,
> and its place remembers it no more.
> But from everlasting to everlasting
> the Lord's love is with those who fear him,
> and his righteousness with their children's children—
> with those who keep his covenant
> and remember to obey his precepts."
> (Psalm 103:15-18)

Do Not Be Afraid

Jesus repeatedly said these four words to His disciples: "Do not be afraid." (Matthew 10:26,28,31, 14:27, 17:7; Luke 8:50, 12:7,32; John 14:27, for example.) But this was nothing new. He was repeating a command God had spoken to His people countless times in the Old Testament (Genesis 46:3; Exodus 14:13, 20:20; Numbers 14:9; Deuteronomy 3:22, 31:6; Joshua 10:8, *etc.*).

If we read the Bible at all, we cannot escape the conclusion that *God does not want us to be afraid*—not of life, not of death, not of other people, not of failure or loss or persecution or criticism. "For God did not give us a spirit of timidity, but a spirit of power, of love and of self-discipline" (II Timothy 1:7).

When we accept His challenge to live without fear, we experience the freedom He intends for us: the freedom to live godly lives in an ungodly world, to march to a heavenly drummer, no matter how out of step we might seem. That's the adventure, and we can enjoy it.

"Peace I leave with you; my peace I give you. I do not give to you as the world gives. Do not let your hearts be troubled and do not be afraid" (John 14:27).

— 9 —

Hiding or Seeking: What's the Difference?

Have you ever owned a cat?

Over the past 20 years, about a dozen cats have wandered in and out of my life. One of the things I've learned about felines is that they are gifted at hiding. If a cat doesn't want to be found, you won't find him.

Even in a tiny apartment, a cat can find a hiding place you didn't even know existed—under the dirty clothes, on top of a high bookcase, in a partly-opened drawer, under the bed—not to mention the innumerable hiding places they can find outdoors. Their incredibly flexible bodies enable them to squeeze into small spaces where you would think it impossible for them to fit.

Not only can a cat find an undiscoverable hiding place, but he can stay hidden as long as he wants to, largely because cats are capable of being so very, very quiet. The American poet Carl Sandburg compared the noiseless movement of a cat to the "sound" of fog rolling ashore off a lake. That's quiet!

Human beings can't match a cat's physical flexibility, but we, too, can become very adept at hiding in the spiritual sense. Like cats, we find clever hiding places. In the last several chapters, we've looked at many of these:

We may hide "under the dresser" so that we can avoid confronting our own shortcomings.

We may hide among our possessions, in our "warehouses," so that they insulate us from the needs and demands around us.

Sometimes we hide in our human relationships, our "photo albums," putting them above all else and persuading ourselves and others that we're being the selfless, devoted individuals God wants us to be.

Or, our hiding place might be our "trophy case" of achievements, which we use to reaffirm our self-worth instead of deriving our sense of value from our relationship to God.

We can even find a hiding place in our own unimportance, staying "outside the voting booth" so that we disavow any responsibility to actively work at knowing and following God's will.

Or, we may try to lose ourselves "among the crowd," carefully molding our thinking and behavior to conform to those around us, lest we stand out and be criticized.

We may dive under our private "bulldozers," letting fear instead of faith dictate the way we live.

Once we find a good hiding place, we can, like cats, remain there very quietly. We can find all sorts of ways to keep from being "discovered," from having to face the challenges of God's Word and His will. We keep a low profile in church, especially when the stewardship chairman calls, or someone invites us to Sunday School, or volunteers are needed for a new project. We stay away from people whose lives reflect deep spiritual commitment so we don't have to be reminded of our own shallowness. We seek out friends and co-workers who reinforce our worldly achievements and values. We stay busy, too busy to find time for reflection and self-understanding.

Cats come out of hiding eventually, though—when they're hungry. Their need for food ultimately compels them to emerge from their hiding places. Similarly, our spiritual hunger, our yearning to know God, cannot be disregarded indefinitely. We can try to hide from His call, but we can't succeed.

Repeat the Question, Please

Just about everyone who has ever been a classroom teacher—whether in an elementary school, high school or college—will recognize this scenario:

Let's say you're an English Composition teacher. You are at the front of the room, explaining the structure of the short story. Maybe from time to time you turn around and jot down key points on the chalkboard. Finally, you ask the class a question: "What are the five main plot elements of a short story?"

None of the students raises his hand to answer, so you call on one who happens to be looking out the window.

"Can you answer that, Rick?"

Startled, Rick jerks his head back in your direction, flushes slightly pink, then adopts a sheepish expression. He glances briefly at the student next to him, who snickers and says, "Earth to Rick. . . .Earth to Rick. . . ."

"Uhmmm. . . ," he begins. "Well. . .mmm. . . .ummm. . . What was the question?" he asks at last.

"Space Cadet," his friend mutters.

Rick hasn't heard a word you've said in the last ten minutes. He's been physically present but mentally absent. He's "hiding" from you in his daydreaming. As a result, not only is he unable to answer the question, he doesn't know what it is!

We're all like Rick sometimes. Just as he's physically present in class, we go through the physical motions of heeding God's call, the motions of religious activity and outward obedience. We appear to be paying attention and to know all the answers, but in reality, we may not even know what the questions are, much less the answers. Hiding in any of the places we've looked at helps us avoid confronting the truly fundamental questions of life, questions about God's role in our lives and His sovereignty; questions about why evil and suffering exist in the world; questions about right *vs.* wrong; questions about our responsibility to others as well as to God.

We know instinctively that the answers to these questions aren't easy, and the questions themselves are troubling, so we avoid them when we can. After all, we tell ourselves, we can get along in our day-to-day lives without having answers to questions like: "Why am I here?", "Why did God let this happen?", "What's right and what's wrong?"

The Bible tells us we cannot hide indefinitely from those questions, though. God confronts us in every aspect of our lives, even through the world He created, challenging us to seek Him as we witness what He has made. "For since the creation of the world God's invisible qualities—his eternal power and divine nature—have been clearly seen, being understood from what has been made, so that men are without excuse" (Romans 1:20).

In all that He has created, God has revealed Himself to man. We can pretend that He doesn't exist; we can deny the part of us that cries out to know Him. But no one can hide from Him.

Those who call themselves atheists or agnostics have to work very hard to maintain their pose of denying God's existence and His sovereignty because everywhere they turn there is evidence of Him. We see Him in the courageous lives of men and women of faith; we see Him when a baby is born, when the sun rises on another day, when a weary and flagging spirit is miraculously renewed by faith. We see Him when ordinary men and women are empowered by His Spirit to do extraordinary things, and we see Him when the first leaves of spring emerge from a barren branch or the first snowflake of winter drifts to earth.

> "But ask the animals, and they will teach you,
> or the birds of the air, and they will tell you;
> or speak to the earth, and it will teach you,
> or let the fish of the sea inform you.
> Which of all these does not know
> that the hand of the Lord has done this?
> In his hand is the life of every creature
> and the breath of all mankind."
> (Job 12:7-10)

We cannot hide from life's important questions—but still we try. Why?

I think even Christians sometimes try to avoid these questions because *surviving in our complex and threatening world occupies center stage.* It takes all our energy and attention just to make ends meet and to fulfill our most basic commitments: juggling the time demands of home and work; keeping our marriages together in the face of countless pressures; providing a stable and nurturing environment for our children; making some financial provision for the future; attending to the needs of our parents as we try to define a role for ourselves as adult children; keeping pace with information and technology lest we find ourselves out of date in a rapidly-changing world.

Is it any wonder we don't feel that we have time and energy left over to address weighty spiritual questions?

Eileen is struggling to make ends meet after her divorce. She has two young children, a second-shift job in a factory, and bills that are always in a neck-and-neck race with her income.

"I don't have time for questions about the meaning of life," she says. "It takes everything I have just to keep my kids fed and make sure they have warm clothes this winter. I have to find a better job, or find a way to go back to school so I can get a better one in the future. I'll worry about religion later; I don't have time for it now."

Eileen doesn't know that by "postponing" her search for God, she's depriving herself of the one unfailing source of hope and encouragement just when she needs it most. Instead of turning to God when she feels that her life is in a shambles, she's shutting Him out.

Eileen's mindset is typical of so many. There's a built-in irony here though: The more we ignore the challenge to deal with life's basic questions, the less able we are to effectively meet the other demands in our lives. If we have no real sense of purpose, no clearly-defined value system, no basic belief system, then life grows increasingly difficult and we feel more and more adrift, tossed about by forces and pressures over which we have less and less control. Our lives manage us, instead of us managing life. We feel disoriented, confused, and victimized by fate instead of excited about what life holds for us. We live in turmoil instead of peace.

Eileen feels alone and overwhelmed as she struggles to fulfill her demanding role as a single parent, even though help is available to her for the asking. God is waiting lovingly and patiently to meet her needs, to guide her parenting role, to help her face the future with optimism. Instead, she remains in hiding and flounders along, fighting to keep away from the edge of despair.

I believe another reason many try to avoid facing up to

life's fundamental questions is that *we want to feel like we are in control of our lives.* We evade questions about God's commandments regarding our daily living and His sovereignty because we aren't willing to relinquish control.

When I was in graduate school, I became engaged in a philosophical discussion, over coffee, with a very wise man who was not only my graduate advisor and one of my professors, but also a good friend. After listening to me ramble on about my dissatisfaction with the way certain aspects of my life were going, he told me, "Your problem is that you want to control everything." I don't even remember what we were talking about at the time, but that one statement has stayed with me for over a decade.

Giving up control is hard for me. One of the strictest disciplines in my Christian life is constantly reminding myself that God is in control. I wrestle with Him continually, trying to snatch back that control, a little bit here, a little bit there. I find myself wanting to control events, outcomes, relationships, even other people's behavior. I can't. Letting go of that control is a demonstration of trust in Him.

My friend Peggy says that she has recently learned a lesson about control in her professional life. For several months she struggled with the question of whether to continue to be self-employed in her marketing and public relations business or to return to the job marketplace and work for someone else. She tried to map out a career plan for herself so that she would feel some sense of control over her future.

"Finally," she told me, "I decided just to trust God's leading and see where He would take me. I was trying too hard, needing too much to be in control. I know God has things for me to do. My job is to remain open to opportunities and go where He leads me."

How many of us are willing, like Peggy, to give God control of our careers? I think most of us are just the opposite; we want as much control as possible, not only in our careers but in our families, our relationships, and certainly in our financial dealings.

Yet God calls us to trust Him, to rely on Him to meet our needs, to depend on His leading. I think we hide from life's important questions because we fear that facing them may mean having to "let go and let God" with all the unanswered questions that implies. We can't relinquish our "right to know" the answers to "how," "why," "when," "where."

Finally, I believe that we avoid the important questions of life because *we have grown callous*. Communications technology has made us immune to the suffering of others; human agony no longer prompts us to search our hearts for answers. We hear statistics about the plight of the elderly or the homeless or the victims of disaster, starvation, or disease, and we no longer feel compelled to ask, "What is my responsibility to the family of mankind?" "Why is there so much evil in the world?" "What can I do to change things?"

Every day, we have only to turn on the television set or open a newspaper to see brutality, violence, and inhumanity. Each day, the media "inoculate" us with a carefully measured dose of human suffering. Our tolerance builds up and suddenly we find that we're no longer distressed by the agony of others. What a terrifying prospect—to think that we can witness suffering and feel no sympathy, no compassion, no urgency to help.

I recently completed a seven-week training course in "Self-defense for Women" at the local community center.

The instructors taught us a variety of techniques for fending off physical attacks as well as precautions for avoiding them.

One of the things they stressed was that if someone attacks you or behaves in a threatening manner, you should yell at the top of your lungs to both startle the attacker and to attract attention. Naturally, we students all assumed that the instructor meant we should yell "Help!" But here's what he said:

"If you are in a threatening situation, yell 'Fire!' "

What? Yell "Fire!" when you're being attacked? That didn't make sense.

He explained it this way: "People don't care if someone else needs help. They'll just look the other way. But if you yell 'Fire!', people will think there's some danger to themselves, and they care a lot more about that than about danger to you."

What a tragic commentary on the callousness of our world! When we become immune to the suffering of others, we have become deaf to God's call to compassion and responsibility. The Apostle Paul's warning to the Hebrews is directed to us as well: "Today, if you hear his voice, do not harden your hearts" (Hebrews 3:7-11). "Encourage one another daily, as long as it is called Today, so that none of you may be hardened by sin's deceitfulness" (3:13).

No matter how creative we become in our efforts to hide from God, we cannot. Too many events around us demand that we, like the cats, ultimately emerge from hiding. Maybe a loved one dies and suddenly we're confronted with difficult questions demanding answers. We meet a person whose inner strength and loving spirit inspire us to renewed commitment. Or maybe our lives become so hopelessly empty that accepting God's sovereignty is the only hope we have.

Fringe Benefits

Throughout the previous chapters, one of the common themes has been that we take a risk when we come out of hiding. We may risk ridicule or criticism, having to change our lifestyle or relationships or even the way we think. We may risk having to grope for painful answers to painful questions. Yet, when we are willing to take those risks, the blessings far outweigh the unknowns. When we come out of hiding and willingly seek the challenges God places before us, we reap His blessings.

What are some of them?

1. We experience the rich fullness of life Jesus promised us.

Jesus promised us riches—treasures of the heart that give life a dimension the world cannot give: Inner peace. A new ability to see the specialness of other people. Serenity. Confidence. Courage. The assurance that when our strength gives out, we have an infinite supply on which to draw to replenish ourselves. Contrast these blessings with the spiritual poverty we see around us every day, as we meet people living lives of despair, loneliness, antagonistic relationships, and uncertainty about whether they matter at all.

2. We receive the power of God to accomplish His work.

Feeling powerless has a demoralizing effect on the human spirit. But, when we accept the challenge of God's call in our lives, and surrender to His power, He enables us to do the work He has for us *and* to surmount the inevitable trials that go with life. He empowers us to love unconditionally, to give unselfishly, to act compassionately, to choose wisely, and to hope unceasingly. We can do so little by ourselves—what joy to know He is ready, willing...and overwhelmingly able to give us the power of His greatness!

3. Our lives have focus and direction.

When you get in your car to go to a friend's house, don't you always make sure you know where it is? When you make a business appointment at an unfamiliar location, don't you normally ask about the best route? We like to know where we're going. Why is it, then, that so many people are willing to live their lives without any directions?

By coming out of hiding, we exchange lives of reacting to what happens around us for lives with a sense of direction, of forward momentum, of purpose. We have work to accomplish for God, not just by doing the things He commands us, but by being the people He calls us to be. He has provided the map—we need to start navigating!

4. We derive an identity that cannot be attained any other way.

Understanding who we are is essential to our spiritual and emotional health. When we stop hiding in the shadows of "poor-me" insignificance, or the spotlight of our accomplishments, or the safety of our relationships, we can embrace our fundamental identity as glorious, unique, important children of God. We can begin to appreciate our own gifts and the gifts of others as we explore the vastness of God's role for us. We can acknowledge our strengths and accept our weaknesses without constantly measuring ourselves against others.

"For Christ's love compels us, because we are convinced that one died for all, and therefore all died. And he died for all, that those who live should no longer live for themselves but for him who died for them and was raised again.

...Therefore, if anyone is in Christ, he is a new creation; the old has gone, the new has come!... And he has committed to us the message of reconciliation. We are therefore Christ's ambassadors, as though God were making his appeal through us" (II Corinthians 5:14-20).

The identity God gives us remains secure even when the circumstances and the people around us change. When our self-image is rooted in His love and faithfulness and His eternal claim on our lives, not in the world's definitions, we become free to accept His offer of the opportunity to be "made great" by the master Craftsman.

This Way to the Dressing Room

Are you wearing camouflage? Like the tiny chameleon, the lizard that changes color in order to blend with its environment, are you working so hard to stay hidden that you're missing out on the adventure of living enthusiastically for Christ?

Fashions and styles change, but camouflage is never in style with God. If we insist on hiding from Him, we cannot experience life with the depth, the excitement, and the daily sense of expectation that He offers us.

We make choices every day about what shirt, what jacket, what blouse, what shoes we'll wear. Are you willing to retire the camouflage gear forever?

There's a risk. We may lose something earthly that we value. We may be hurt, physically or emotionally or psychologically. People may say unkind things about us. We may get tired.

But we'll be living the only adventure worth giving our lives for. We'll be the ones who, like Isaiah say, "Here am I. Send me!" (Isaiah 6:8). We'll be the ones, like my cousin Bob, living on the edge of silver wings.

"For God who said, 'Let light shine out of dark-

ness', made his light shine in our hearts to give us the light of the knowledge of the glory of God in the face of Christ. But we have this treasure in jars of clay to show that this all-surpassing power is from God and not from us.

We are hard pressed on every side, but not crushed; perplexed, but not in despair; persecuted, but not abandoned; struck down, but not destroyed.... Therefore we do not lose heart" (II Corinthians 4:6-16).

That's the difference between hiding and seeking.